KRAYZY DAYS

Micky Fawcett

Pen Press

First published in Great Britain by Pen Press

All paper used in the printing of this book has been made from wood grown in managed, sustainable forests.

ISBN: 978-1-78003-525-3

Printed and bound in the UK
Pen Press is an imprint of
Indepenpress Publishing Limited
25 Eastern Place
Brighton
BN2 1GJ

A catalogue record of this book is available from
the British Library

Cover design by Jacqueline Abromeit

Steve 'Legs' Diamond
– RIP Legs

CONTENTS

INTRODUCTION

We were going to kill Reggie Kray. I had a .38 revolver and we were waiting for him late one night outside John Bigg Point, a block of flats in Stratford, East London. Reggie and I had once been close and for years I knew the Kray twins as well as anyone. But now their world was in disarray. They were lost in their own celebrity; a fame which brought with it a circle of yes-men and hangers-on. Wannabe gangsters who fuelled brother Ronnie's madness. Only a few of us who had been around for longer could see the twins were heading for disaster. If we didn't do anything they would take us down with them.

I had begun planning to hit the Krays not long after Ronnie shot George Cornell dead in The Blind Beggar pub. Cornell was a member of a rival gang and the Krays had a deadly feud with them, but even so, Ronnie wasn't going to get away with killing him in front of so many witnesses. I made the decision to walk away from the Krays and I took a few of my trusted friends with me.

That night when Reggie left the club to take a girlfriend home, I received a coded telephone call. It was all prearranged. We had to go after them as soon as we saw an opportunity. Cutting myself off from the Krays made me a marked man. Getting them first struck me then as only logical, but the truth was that I was under almost as much pressure as the twins. My own grasp on reality was slipping as I sat in a car in the shadows and believed I could shoot Reggie Kray and get away with it. I just felt that I didn't have a choice.

I no longer recognised Reggie as the man I first met when I was starting to make a name for myself in the East End underworld. Back then the Krays had almost established their empire and I learned a lot. Reggie was quick to show his approval of the way

1

I became a successful conman by targeting big-time fences. I became a trusted ally in the Krays' own business frauds – schemes we called long firms. I always kept my independence but we had some fun together.

One of my earliest memories of the twins was Ronnie in expansive mood in their immaculate London club, The Double R. One of the many venues they ran, it was done out with flock wallpaper, it had an attractive bar and it was well run. That made it popular and this was a typical night. There were a few cars parked outside in Bow Road and their owners were inside with a drink while a Dean Martin-ish singer called Lenny Pugh was crooning a rendition of *Volare* on the mic. Couples were dotted around enjoying the relaxed atmosphere.

Ronnie hadn't long been home from Long Grove, a mental hospital in Surrey. That night he was at his smartest. Suit, collar and tie and shoes so shiny you could see your face in them. As Reggie wasn't around that evening it fell to Ronnie to be the genial host and he was scrupulous in doing so. He worked the whole room, picking out couples from the regular punters to thank them personally for coming along and adding, 'I hope you have a pleasant evening.' As if they didn't know, he told them that he ran the place with his brothers Reggie and Charlie and if there was anything they needed, anything at all, they should just let him know.

Completing a whole circuit of the club, Ronnie ended up back at the entrance. Tony Lucraft, a tough guy from Hoxton, was perched on a low leather sofa near the door.

'Hello, Tony, I didn't see you sitting there,' Ronnie said politely. He paused as if some explanation were needed for this lapse in greeting etiquette. Both twins were short-sighted. 'I've got bad eyes, you know,' he added.

'You must have fucking bad eyes, Ron,' said Tony. 'I've been sitting here for 20 minutes.'

You had to judge your moment with Ronnie. Tony might have thought that in the relaxed atmosphere he could get away with a smart comment. But without hesitation and in full view of the ordinary customers, Ronnie immediately smashed him in the face before kicking him off the sofa and attempting to stamp on him. The barman and the door staff, big men hired by the Krays to keep the place going, ran up but even with their combined muscle still

2

Ronnie could only be pulled off his victim when they promised to throw him out. Cabaret concluded, Ronnie began another circuit of the bar, still panting and sweating from the brutal assault. He spoke to all the same couples as if the extreme violence had been no more of an inconvenience than running out of a draft beer at the bar.

'I'm terribly sorry about that,' he repeated to each guest, still slightly out of breath. 'It doesn't happen very often.'

This wasn't the first time I'd met Ronnie, though he had been away a long time and in that time I had got to know his brother better. Reggie was more predictable, a bit less volatile. He was also much more uptight, focused on business, but I never felt safe around either of them.

I had long been aware of the Krays before I met any of them. We had lived in the same area and we had had a similar sort of upbringing. We all grew up during the Second World War and I also managed to get myself out of National Service – though not, I have to admit, in as spectacular fashion as they did when they got themselves dishonourably discharged for extremely bad behaviour. For me, school was no more of an attraction than it had been for them and like them I was never attracted by the world of straight work. I could handle myself in a fight and it wasn't long before I met them as I made my way in the criminal world. We got on and I won myself a reputation, though I don't say that to glorify our lifestyle. Looking back at what we all used to do actually makes me feel queasy. I see all of us around the twins drifting along a sea of booze, spending money as fast as we got it and living from day to day. I look back on it with a sort of horror now. And yet I don't want to come over like one of those Sicilian *penitenti*, an ex-gangster sorry for everything he's done. I'd like to tell my story straight.

The Krays knew me as Mick, never Mike or Michael. And yes, we were friendly. But I was never in what the endless accounts of the Krays always call the firm – or rather, Firm, always with a capital F. I don't recognise the Krays I knew from what I've read. I'm not sure there was a firm at all. They started out fairly disorganised and it never really changed, despite what the press would have you believe about protection rackets and the like.

I came into their orbit along with what was known as the Queen's Road mob. This was a collection of gangsters operating out of Upton Park, east of Kray territory. Crime in London was strictly divided by district. Tight-knit crews operated in each area with their own hierarchy of criminals and when they weren't feuding most of them never mixed with their neighbours. I got to know the crews in nearby Canning Town – we all knew of each other, at least, even if most of us never strayed from our home turf. The Krays didn't.

I was always more independent than most. I made friends over the Thames around the Elephant & Castle. I made sure I was not too close to the Krays but I always appeared loyal. I got to see the personal side of them that they did their best to keep hidden. When Frances – beautiful, tragic Frances, Reggie's doomed wife – said that their marriage wasn't consummated, she said it to me in front of Reggie. And when Reggie later suspected she was seeing someone else he asked me to sort it out. And I was right in the centre of the story that brought them down – the killing of George Cornell. He was never killed because he called Ronnie a poof. That was just a legend we created to hide the truth of a feud gone desperately wrong. The reality was the twins were trying to buy themselves time. They turned to me to help them.

They were terrible with business. The Krays were all smoke and mirrors and the press went along with it. I was never one of the yes-men who surrounded them in increasing numbers as they became famous. I was more restrained, or at least I liked to think so. I didn't have the bloodlust the twins developed. Of course, it's not too difficult to be saner than the next man if the next man is a Kray. And it's even easier when the other next man is his twin brother. The sanity bar is not exactly raised high. By walking away I issued a challenge and that's how I ended up sitting outside a block of flats with a revolver, waiting for Reggie. By then I even believed I might take his place. You see what I mean about sanity being relative? More than a few people certainly thought I was completely fucking mad. These days I can see why. I was a strange mix of the very cautious and the utterly reckless.

I made my money by targeting other criminals in complicated and elegant frauds. But I made sure I covered my tracks and I never looked for publicity like the Krays did. I was smarter and as a result, extremely self-confident. Arrogant, if you like. I spent all the money I got; I drank all the time and I got into fights. Sometimes I took people by surprise as I was never a big bloke. I was softly spoken and it was only after winning a couple of legendary fights that I began to get a reputation for being dangerous. Everyone began to hear I would use a weapon if I had to and before long I began to believe my own press and span out of control. I never actually killed anyone, but I came close. I always loved French gangster movies and in the end I felt like I was a character in one of them.

But everyone knows how this story ends. I didn't shoot Reggie dead. Nobody did. All three Kray brothers died in prison. So you might think I'm making it all up. But think about this. I'm in my 70s now and it's a bit late to start making a name for myself. So why this book? Why now?

There are already quite enough books about the Krays and London's underworld. I've seen quite a lot of them myself. But most of them are full of lies or just plain wrong – I can't finish most of them, I get that annoyed. I look myself up in the index but I don't recognise much of what I read as being anywhere near the truth. Now I want to set the record straight.

I'm not going to tell the same old stories you can find in countless other accounts, but I am going to tell you what it was like to be part of the Krays' intimate circle, to know them on a daily basis, to drink with them – if not exactly to relax with them.

I didn't want to talk before and it hasn't been easy doing it now. I've found myself not wanting to reveal the truth. I can't shake that instinct of self-preservation I've always had. But I've made the decision to say what really happened and I'm not going to go back on it.

Operating independently of the twins I knew their characters and I was there to see the myths being created. It's incredible to think how much longer the legends have lasted than the years the twins were at large. Most of what happens in this book concerning the twins took place over just a few years – around 1957 to 1967. That was as tense and dangerous a period as it was brief, but because the twins became so famous you think of them being in the public eye for longer than that. Such an adrenaline-fuelled life couldn't last. I know I was lucky to get out when I did.

I stopped drinking in the 1970s and I calmed down a lot, though I never did quite go straight. I still had opponents, though they changed considerably over the years. In the 1980s I became a boxing trainer and faced down another tight mob – the promoters who controlled every aspect of the sport. Gangsters without guns, as someone called them. And yet my most recent opponent, you might be surprised to hear, was not a fighter of any kind, but a figure in the world of art. Banksy is the end of my story, but maybe he's also a good place to begin.

His representatives took exception when I got involved in selling reproductions of his famous London graffiti and we started battling – though through lawyers rather than on the streets. It was a vicious fight all the same. My side wanted me to throw in the towel from the start, but I wasn't having any of it. Who was this man who never put his face to the artwork he made? It intrigued me. I thought Banksy's reticence might be my best chance at beating him. I'd spent my whole life doing everything I could to keep out of the limelight and I had a hunch that he would do the same. My barrister sent a letter which opened with the knockout question. *'Who is this man?'* If he wanted to take us to court, we were going to unmask him. The challenge worked out beautifully – we never heard from them again. Now I've finally decided to come out of the shadows and if I'm going to be honest I've got to answer that same question about myself. It's not been easy to talk about an underworld life I've always had to hide. But now I need to answer the question we put to Banksy.

Who is this man?

Chapter One

THE DOUBLE R

Ronnie Kray gave Hoxton villain Tony Lucraft such a beating in The Double R Club I expected him to make himself scarce. I was surprised to see Tony pop up just a few days later for Ronnie's birthday when there was a gathering in the local billiard hall. I didn't know the victim myself but his bruises and swollen face made him unmistakeably the man from the earlier night.

Tony not only gave Ronnie a present, but had it wrapped up nicely as well. I was so astonished I still remember what it was. A jumper. This was carefully unpacked by Ronnie and held up for general admiration. The scene of heart-warming cosiness was completed by the deadpan conversation between the two.

'I hope you like it,' said Tony.

'Oh, yes,' said Ronnie in a distant monotone. 'It's very nice. Yes. Thank you, Tony. Thank you.'

Beatings such as the one that Ronnie gave Tony were not unusual and they were generally just as quickly forgotten in the world of the Kray twins. There was the ex-boxer from Holloway who hadn't seen Ronnie for a while. Ronnie was in La Monde, a Chelsea nightclub, following a trip to work on a scheme in Nigeria when the boxer unwisely patted Ronnie's midriff and commented, 'Cor! You've put on a bit of weight, haven't you?' Ronnie had acquired a massive African knife as a souvenir, which was, as with all of his weapons, being held by a trusted colleague. It was swiftly retrieved and the boxer regretted his light-hearted comment.

Drunken brawls, feuds and slights – imagined and real – fuelled London's underworld. Professional gangsters running firms like City corporations existed only in the movies. Yet there was a real difference between us and the normal world, the straight people. We kept ourselves apart from regular people. The Krays were scared of their law-abiding fellow Londoners, that was the truth. There was a separate set of rules and a hierarchy for us. Money was made, lots of it on occasions. But none of it was kept. There was no guiding intelligence behind what the Krays did and they very quickly reached their limits. They were unwilling or unable to graduate beyond the streets in which they grew up. And like them, I lived apart from the straight world and at the same time spent much of my time in the same places as the people I knew all my life.

The Krays were born in Hoxton – Ronnie and Reggie in 1933, Charlie in 1926. I came from further east, down by the Thames in Silvertown. I was born a few years after Ronnie and Reggie, two doors from the docks in 1937. We were right next to where City Airport is now. The authorities said my family were in real danger when the Second World War broke out a couple of years later, the same year that my younger brother was born. The docks were a prime target for the German Luftwaffe and we were moved nearby. Custom House is just around the corner, but we didn't stay long. An incendiary bomb fell on the house and, perhaps not surprisingly, provided me with my first memory as a very young child.

My grandfather was Thomas McKeown, a labourer from Cork who moved to New York where he met Margaret Riordan. They married in the old St Patrick's Cathedral in New York and ended up in London after my grandfather had to go looking for work. I still have a cousin in the States – same age as me. My grandparents had two boys called Mallachy and Thomas and a girl, my mum, called Margaret. She married Frederick Fawcett and they must have liked the names because they called my brother Frederick and one of my sisters was Margaret. The other was named Brenda. And in another name coincidence, my sister Margaret and my American cousin, Margaret McKeown, both went on to marry men called David Fitzgerald.

My dad, Frederick, born in 1907, was a merchant seaman at one time, but by the time war broke out he had been a soldier for seven years. With his experience he was made a sergeant in the King's

Royal Rifle Corps and became a regimental drill instructor for the Officer Cadet Training Unit (OCTU) in Winchester. It meant he was in charge of all the would-be officers. By the end of the war he'd been a soldier for 12 years in all. I didn't get to know him until he returned. In Custom House it was just my mum and my brother – my sisters didn't arrive until after Dad got back.

Aside from the bomb, I always remember that we never had many visitors to our house. My parents didn't invite people, it was just like that. I grew up to be the same as an adult, not very good at mixing and I like my privacy. When the whole of the media and celebrity world seemed to turn around the Krays, I'd be much happier in the West End or places like Paris and Hamburg where you could go and spend a nice few quid without attracting any attention. It probably helped the twins to realise they could trust me – I wouldn't be talking to journalists. If anything, they were the worst for fraternising with the media. Even today, I'm still nervous at the prospect of inviting people into my own home. This has its roots in straightforward anti-Irish feeling. Neighbours in Custom House couldn't even pronounce my mum's surname and they regarded us with suspicion. I was determined not to pass on that trait when I had my own family and I succeeded. My son gets on with anyone and life for him has been different and easier as a result.

I only have dim memories of my grandparents, they were already very old when I was born, but I know that Thomas had a reputation for fighting. In that way he lived up to the Irish stereotype, my mother told me that where they lived in Custom House he had a right good fight in the street with local hero and one time world bantam weight champion, Pedlar Palmer. That was something else I inherited, along with a love of drinking that lasted for years. Everyone drank when I was a young man. That went with the territory.

The neighbours in Custom House weren't sorry to see us bombed out by the incendiary. Mum got us temporarily housed in rest centres and that gave me another lasting memory – the nit comb. That was the first thing they'd do to me when I went into those places, scrape the horrible metal teeth of the comb through my hair. Fortunately we weren't homeless for too long. Dad was doing well as a drill instructor in Winchester and he was able to get us billeted in the deanery in the grounds of the cathedral. Mum was given a job helping out the cook. It was a peaceful home, the building itself dating back some 300 years or more, parts of it even older. There was weaponry stored there by the armed forces – I remember jumping up on a table to pose with a rifle once – but mostly the place had been left as it was before the war, down to the furnishings and the silverware. That gave me an early taste of what it was like to enjoy graceful living. And it also made me feel like an outsider again, just as I had in Custom House.

I found it hard to settle when we got back to the East End. I never really felt comfortable anywhere. Silvertown, the area in which I'd been born, was drab in comparison to cathedral life. There was nothing there at all, apart from a pub and one old cinema. A strange place, Silvertown almost seemed to be in the River Thames itself. Behind its streets you could see moored cargo ships rising up and, if you didn't know the river was there, it looked like as if they might have been somehow parked on a road behind. It was the industrial heart of the river and for me a return to East London wasn't a homecoming. I was never going to be a typical East Ender. That's probably why I got on so well with the other children in Winchester. We chirpy little Londoners were fussed over by adults with names such as Trollope-Bellew. They emphasised the importance of good manners and showed us a different world. But I also saw how war was a class leveller for many of those toffs who went off to fight as officers and never came back.

In the relatively short time me and my brother spent in Winchester, our accents changed. We ended up speaking quite nicely – though we soon lost that when we came back. I've since always spoken like a typical cockney, not gruff, but all the same you'd never have known I was ever in such a refined city.

We eventually settled a few miles to the north in Stratford where my mum rented a house. I went to a primary school around the corner from which I was expelled for fighting. I wasn't a bad kid but I was into boxing and that led to trouble. After Mum got a radio I listened to the sport all the time. I was also addicted to comedy like *ITMA* (*It's That Man Again*) and Charlie Chester and drama like *Dick Barton: Special Agent*, but the boxing would be a lifelong love. Much later I would even end up as a trainer.

I hadn't got into fights at school, though I never felt that I was particularly liked. There was no real reason for anyone not to get on with me, it was just that feeling I had of being an outsider. And I think grandfather Thomas's fighting spirit was already in me. I ended up punching a few boys as if I was practising boxing with them. But when I hit another lad on the nose – and we were all just little kids – the teacher went mad. Usually you'd get the stick on your hand but he made me bend over and gave me four good whacks with the cane. Then we got the letter outlining the other schools I could go to. I think the fact that I was a Catholic and it was a Protestant school had something to do with the severity of the punishment.

I went to a Catholic school called St Anthony's at the other side of West Ham Park. Now I was in Forest Gate rather than Stratford and I quite liked it at the new place. I had a good teacher who was Scottish, Mr Connelly. But I was only there for a year before I went a couple of roads south to St Bonaventure's. This was the only Catholic grammar school in the area and it was known for being good. Kids came from all over the East End to get in there – from Custom House in the south to Tilbury in Essex. St Bonaventure's was also a technical and modern school and I fitted in more with those kids even though I was a grammar boy. My contemporaries were much posher and their fathers were invariably headmasters themselves. We were taught by Franciscan brothers and many years later I ran into my old form master, Father Andrew. He didn't remember me but when I told him which class I'd been in he told me about the rest of the class.

'Did you know Michael Cola is now a professor? Clark is a psychiatrist.'

By then I was 30-something and up to my neck in trouble. But I wasn't surprised to hear what happened to the rest of them – we even used to call Cola 'professor' in class.

My school used to produce a national boxing champion each year and the sport continued to obsess me. That was the big thing for lads then – it was as popular as football is now. I was a schoolboy boxer myself and I really enjoyed it, though I came to realise I would never make it as a professional fighter. I haven't really got the physique, I'm not built strongly and I haven't got the reflexes. Someone once said to me that all I had in boxing was the desire to do it. That ambition was a help when I later went into the training side of the sport. But even with my limited talent I won most of my fights – I scooped the West Ham borough championship and then the Essex county championship.

I trained at West Ham Boxing Club – they had so many of the British professional champions, boxers like Terry Gill and Terry Spinks, the Olympic gold medallist – and I knew them all. I grew up with them. We were in the same team. But I couldn't keep up. As lads get older they should become stronger and I just didn't develop in the right way. Yet even though it was clear I was never going to get to the next level, I did have two very close fights with a boy who was runner-up in the national championships. But styles make fighters. That's the only rule in boxing and my style was too basic. I was okay if my opponent came straight at me. I knew what to do – put my chin down, keep my shoulders up and march forward, punching left and right. But if the other fella boxed properly – had a decent jab and good footwork– I wouldn't know what to do. I'm slow. It wasn't just my build and technique. When I realised that I wasn't going to make it I stopped training so hard and in my late teens I had a fight in which I was knocked out. By then I had discovered booze and birds and I was little more than a fan of the sport.

It was through boxing that I first saw the Kray name in print – Reggie appeared in a book of East London boxing results called *The Straight Left*. The twins were five years older than me and already well into their careers by the time I started. Reggie lost to a fella called Laurie Gold. Like me the twins were initially disciplined before losing interest. Another boy making his name as a fighter came from the year above me: Roy Shaw from Barking, later a London legend in his own right. He was never part of the Krays' circle though, he always stood alone. I knew him as Shawry when we became friends years later, though he later got the nickname Pretty Boy. That must have been much later! I don't know who dreamed that one up. I liked his sense of humour but he was always a bit full on, very intense.

Schoolwork took a back seat to boxing. That was always my excuse – I didn't learn anything; I didn't do anything else. I'd always be saying, 'I've got to go practise boxing,' and that was it. With such a good record in the sport, the school didn't push me on the academic side. The teachers made it clear they thought I wasn't going anywhere and why should they care? They had the likes of Cola the future professor and Clark the psychiatrist. When I told them I couldn't keep up and wanted to do woodwork they were quick to oblige and I was soon back with the mob from Custom House. I didn't like those kids any better and I was useless at woodwork. I just didn't want to do anything. Nothing. I didn't aim higher than being the milk monitor. It gave me more time to smoke fags. I left at 15 without sitting any exams.

My parents didn't know anything about this. They were hard workers. They worked until they dropped. They were too busy to notice anything, certainly not what was going on at school and they had my sisters to think about too – both of them came along more than ten years after me. My brother was still at school and they needed to provide for all of them.

I had no wish to follow my parents' example. Dad had come out of the forces after the war and he was a pitch navvy. His job involved clambering down into these enormous metal containers. They had been used for storing pitch and at the bottom was a thick, black residue which he would break up with a pickaxe. On sunny days it would get very hot in those barrels and pitch gave off toxic fumes. It was killing him – even I could see that. He got to the point where he couldn't physically do it and he became a gatekeeper for big institutions like factories and hospitals. That was very much his kind of thing – he still carried himself like a military man, upright and imposing and he looked the part for doing security. He was also a drinker and the regular hours fitted in with the pub. My mum worked in factories all her life. There wasn't much alternative. There were factories everywhere and those were the only jobs that you got to hear about.

Neither of my parents had much choice in their careers but they hadn't expected to get any. They just didn't know any better and there was never anyone at their schools asking them what they wanted out of life. My destiny should have been the same and to begin with it was. My first job was at the Tate & Lyle sugar refinery in Silvertown – which still operates near City Airport. Not knowing any different, I didn't mind the job. The wages were good – four pounds and 16 shillings a week and my parents were happy with that. Theirs had been a truly poverty-stricken background – what was called a no-shoes upbringing. The height of their ambition was that you kept your job.

Most people in our area had that worker mentality. There wasn't anything else. So when you spoke about friends and family it was just in terms of how good their work was – which factory they were at, how much they were being paid, how secure it was. Apart from me – I didn't subscribe to that. I'd seen Mum coming in from work pulling little spikes of steel out of her hands because she was on a lathe all day making pressed hinges. And that wasn't even anything particularly hard for the times. Most of our friends and family accepted their lot but watching them suffer turned me off work. I didn't even last at Tate & Lyle for three months. They'd taken on loads of young school leavers and then stood them all off. None of us had done anything wrong and I was even more disillusioned.

That said, I went back six months later and got a job on the docks, working on the raw sugar landing, unloading sugar from the barges. But like most of my jobs it was short-lived and I heard that the really good money was to be had in lagging pipes with asbestos covering. My parents – for all their belief in working until you couldn't do it any more – did me a right favour in warning me off. They knew the health risks. All the kids who did that are dead now of asbestosis. Every single one of them. My parents also warned me off Hemingway & Co, a factory on what's now the site of the Olympic park. They used toxic materials like arsenic.

Outside of work I didn't do much. Me and my mates would wander the streets and go to the pictures on a Sunday afternoon. I wasn't into anything in particular – though we did go to a youth club sometimes and we were all into boxing. As we got older we began to venture further afield, going up to the West End of London, but that was about it for entertainment.

Queen's Road Market changed everything. The market was down Queen's Road off Green Street in Upton Park, not far from where I lived. I met a fella called Jonah on the market who introduced me to the nearest I've ever seen to the American model of the Mafia. It was all based around illegal gambling, fruit and vegetables and every kind of crooked business imaginable, which sounds unlikely now. But there were always four or five bookies on the square at the top of the market taking bets and rationing meant that fresh food was at a premium after the war. The market stall game was a good earner and you had to be prepared to throw your weight around if you wanted in. The big stalls were run by families and their lavish displays were like those you regularly get in supermarkets now. We'd never seen bananas as kids and all of a sudden there was all this produce in abundance. The traders themselves all had cars – and their families had everything they wanted – but they were terrible bullies and they were crooked. The whole street market was in on the gambling. They even had a system of whistles to let everyone know when a policeman was coming along.

Quite a few of them on the market were Jewish and they had moved out from the true East End around Aldgate. I don't know the history of Upton Park and how the Jews came to be there, but it became the centre of my world when I got a job standing on fruit stalls. I ended up working on one pitch outside The Queen's pub – mine wasn't one of the biggest, but I was just happy to be a part of market life. The work was much more enjoyable than the factory jobs and I liked playing up to the image of being a barrow boy.

My job ended when The Queen's, owned by a friendly old man called Izzy Miller, changed hands. I never knew what actually happened – either the new owner decided he didn't want the stall outside his place, or local government, which was always on the case of anyone who'd infringed one rule or other, decided that the stall took up too much of the pavement. Whatever the reason, I was about to be out of work. But not for long. I'd got to know people in the area and made a good impression on them. They could see I had proved myself and there were always people who looked out for you and could introduce you to someone else in the neighbourhood. Another stallholder, Wolfy Lowery, had his eye on me.

'You looking for a job?'

'Yeah, I am now.' This brief exchange was the beginning. This was my first step into a new world.

Wolfy was as good as his word. He introduced me to Leon Kaiser and the Sohn brothers, Maurice and Jack, more Jewish guys, who ran a warehouse in Aldgate: Textile & Haberdashery Auctions Ltd. I was an impressionable 17-year-old and I could hardly believe that one of my new bosses had a yellow Rolls Royce. The Sohns also went under the names Mr Maurice and Mr Jackson. Even I could tell they were a bit warm, though I didn't know their entire operation was crooked. I wouldn't have cared if I had – it was lively! Exciting. I still remember the address: 2 The Minories, Aldgate. Magical words. What a bustling, exciting area. The firm auctioned off clothing material and food and sweets on alternate fortnights and I never found out where they got it from. I didn't ask any questions, I just pulled on my brown coat and boots and unloaded the gear from the lorry.

'Ain't you heard of Sonny the Yank?' asked one of the brothers. I hadn't. 'He's Jack Spot's right-hand man.'

'Who's Jack Spot?'

'Never heard of Jack Spot?' The Sohns had a unique way of explaining things and they painted me a vivid picture. 'Listen, you know when a business employs someone to carry their moneybag chained to his wrist to the bank? They don't when Sonny's around. He'll chop the hand off.'

It was a typical piece of invention but it made the point. The Sohns knew Sonny and he worked for Jack Spot, one of those London legends every wannabe gangster modelled themselves after. He was a hero too – he fought Oswald Mosely's fascist blackshirts in the Battle of Cable Street.

The Sohns had impressed me just as much as they intended – but they also got me thinking. And it was when I got back to Upton Park and I started looking around. The fellas who drank in The Queen's. The market traders. Everyone working around me. They were all gangsters. It was like a light had suddenly gone on. And another followed soon after when I learned that you didn't even need to be a criminal to get in trouble with the police. One night I was out for a walk with a couple of mates around Edgware Road and we weren't doing anything at all. These big plain-clothed coppers just grabbed us and threw us in the back of a car. It was terrifying and no less so when they eventually identified themselves as the Flying Squad from Scotland Yard. We'd committed no crime but that's how it was – the police didn't need much provocation to pull you off the street.

We got taken to Paddington Green nick and slung in a cell and it was ages before I finally fell asleep. In the middle of the night the police came back for me and demanded to know where we were going, what we were doing.

'We were just having a walk around!' I insisted. And that was absolutely true. We'd never been to that area and we were just there for something to do. They told me to sign for the items they said they'd found in my pockets, I refused – a knife and a car door handle – neither of which were mine. I couldn't even drive at the time and I'd have had no idea how to pinch a car. Why would I keep the door handle anyway? I found out what they were up to the next day when I was charged with being a 'suspected person' loitering with intent to commit an offence and being armed with an offensive weapon. I'd done no such thing but that was no defence. They had me under the hated 'sus' (for suspected person) law that they've since done away with – the one they used to nick loads of black men. The police thought they could do anything until there were riots when minority communities decided they weren't going to put up with it any more.

My parents might not have been so concerned with what was happening at school, but this got their attention. My dad went mad. Neither of them could believe that they were going to have to come to court with me. Fortunately, my new friend Sonny came to my assistance. When I told him what had happened he was calm and unruffled.

'Oh, go and see my solicitor,' he said. 'Ask for Bernard Perkoff and tell him I sent you.'

He was right not to be worried. The solicitor tore the police to bits, while the two detective sergeants sat in court with their heads in their hands. They'd got us for no good reason and must have thought we'd be an easy way to get the arrest numbers up. Now they shifted and squirmed as they were taken apart by us nobodies. Then the magistrate came to the verdict and after much thought he found us guilty. But then he added, 'Conditional discharge.' He wasn't actually going to go against the police – that wasn't the done thing in a police court. They all knew each other and the magistrate wasn't going to step on police toes. That was the way it worked and once I had a bit of experience myself I knew what to expect.

But I already knew that I didn't mind being in court. More than that, in a strange way I liked it. Here was a taste of a different life – from the buzz of the Aldgate place, to being recommended a solicitor by Sonny and getting one over on the police. We hadn't entirely got away with it but it had been exciting. At last I had found something I could really get into. That's what finally made sense when I found out that all those fellas down Queen's Road were gangsters. I got on with my work and in return they looked out for me. This was a world that I instinctively felt comfortable in and they recognised me as a like-minded person.

But before I had a chance to start my new life in earnest I got my papers. National Service. It was September 1955 and I resolved to go in quickly and get it over and done with as fast as possible. That same morning a newspaper board caught my eye on the way to work: MAN SERIOUSLY STABBED IN WEST END BRAWL. I thought to myself, I bet that's Jack Spot! The man that the Sohns talked about. I'd had a chance to meet him when he and Sonny made one of their regular visits to the auctions. I only knew him in passing, but I was convinced he was the one in the story – and I was right. The people in whose world I was just starting to move were right in the middle of major trouble – and I had to go in the army. I was even less inclined to do my National Service.

But there was nothing for it. I got through the medical and was posted down to Portsmouth for six weeks of square bashing – drilling and that sort of thing. They decided that if I fitted in anywhere I would be a corporal and I got sent to Blackdown. I didn't want to be a corporal, of course, and I didn't want to be in Blackdown either –I had more friends over the road at Deepcut. But nobody was going to listen to me. I was in the First Battalion RAOC and we were sent to Bordon Camp. A waste of time. I thought so and so did a new friend from Liverpool – Jerry White: Scouse White.

Like me, Jerry had been a schoolboy boxer. We filled our time in the army gym, sparring, running together in the morning and waiting until we could go to the cookhouse, then waiting until the evening. When the village pub opened we'd go for a drink and – well, nothing else. There was nothing happening. At least when the weekend finally did drag itself along we could go home. A coach took me back to London where I was allowed 36 hours with my family. I would usually go out on the town on a Saturday night before heading back. The routine never varied and I hated it.

I was feeling increasingly desperate and a fellow recruit gave me some tips for getting out. What I was going to do would need practice, but I was determined. Step one was to complain of having headaches. It was duly noted. I waited for a while before choosing step number two. We had to attend an officer commanding (OC) parade which meant yet more drilling and this, I decided, would be my way out. I told a fellow recruit from Highbury and Islington in London what I was going to do just beforehand. But as we clattered down the stairs in our army boots on our way to the parade grounds I felt my courage drain away with every step.

'You've given me all that fucking mouth about what you're going to do,' the kid from Highbury hissed at me, 'and you ain't going to fucking do it? No!' This was the encouragement I needed.

'All right, I'll show you,' I said.

As we got in formation I walked sideways up to a corporal who totally ignored me as he gazed out over the parade ground, at all the new soldiers and the sergeant major. I hit him on the chin. Completely unsuspecting, he went down at once but soon staggered back to his feet and was about to get at me. Other recruits got in the way.

'Hold tight, hold tight!' they told him.

I stared at the corporal. 'He was laughing at me!'

Well, he wasn't. He wasn't even looking at me. This caused much consternation among my superiors. What was to be done with me? My erratic behaviour, taken with the headaches, was enough to get me referred to Hut 25, Stills Road, Aldershot – the army psychiatrist.

'Would you be happy if I recommended you for discharge?' he asked me. This was step three and the fella who had been coaching me had told me exactly how to respond.

'Yes!' I said. This was the point at which most people messed up. If you tried to make out you didn't really want to get out then they would keep you on. You couldn't pretend to be loyal. You had to be definite about it. It worked. The psychiatrist wrote up his report and I was out, marked down as 'temperamentally unstable', with a huge smile on my face and the assault on the corporal behind me.

During my brief time in the army the Aldgate auction warehouse had closed down after Leon Kaiser skipped to America with all the money. I went back to life down Queen's Road where, after work had finished for the day, a lot of the locals would go out drinking. They were known as the Queen's Road mob and nobody interfered with them. Now I got my first proper brush with gangster families and I loved it. Part of the Queen's Road strength came from everyone being very clannish, all seemingly related to each other. Daughters-of would marry sons-of. It was an exclusive club and I was determined to find my way in. The key was not to be a nuisance. Just stay on the right side of them and earn their trust slowly. I liked what I saw of them. They were unmistakable – confident, flashy, smart and they always had money. It looked like an exciting life.

Crime bosses Jack Spot and Billy Hill – who were partners for a while and controlled a large portion of London's crime – drew a lot of their supporters from the Queen's Road. They also had another crew who were Bobby Warren, Battles Rossi, Billy Bly, Frankie Fraser and co. Jack and Billy made sure they were friendly with everyone – that was how they became successful. North, south and Upton Park – everywhere was under their control, except the East End. There wasn't really a distinct criminal fraternity in that area then, not in the sense of something around Mile End. That would come with the Krays who were Jack Spot's protégés at the time.

Billy had a lot of interests in West End gambling, while Jack Spot never set his sights as high. Spot would always go the criminal route. He'd never pay for anything if he could avoid it, while Billy bought himself a luxurious, tasteful lifestyle in London and he had a reputation – which wasn't really that accurate – for being refined. After their split, Jack didn't manage to hang on to his position and everyone set about him. It left Billy Hill the undisputed top figure in London.

Jack and Billy were as well known as the Krays. They were more successful, smarter and Billy Hill, in particular, was more discreet. He would end up playing a big part in my life. He was more thoughtful than the twins, more considered and was always able to think a few steps ahead. The Krays knew it and they hated it. Their ambition and lust for glory always outstripped their abilities and Billy made fools of them.

Some of the faces on a Monday night in The Queen's pub were serious names in their own right: Jacky Reynolds, Teddy Machin, Georgie and Jimmy Woods, who had served long sentences for a major robbery at Heathrow Airport. Porky Bennett was another. He had got eight years PD (preventative detention) for slashing a wrestler with a razor in a restaurant in the old Chinese neighbourhood around Limehouse. I would later have a run in with his family myself. Georgie Woods and Jacky Reynolds would go on to run The Spieler for the twins. Among the Queen's Road mob were also those who would venture over the water – meaning over the Thames – to around the Elephant & Castle area. This was the crowd I felt at home with. I was watching the way they made sure they knew people all over London and it was through them that I first heard about a new venue – a club called The Double R.

Chapter Two

THE JARS AND THE CORNER

I started making serious money by being a conman. And the best people to con are other criminals. Big ones – fences. This is how it works. It all relies on the intro – a mutual acquaintance they can't and usually don't want to contact because, greedily, it would mean giving them a cut of their profits. 'Listen,' I would say, 'so and so told me to contact you. I've just done a robbery and it looks like it's come on top for me. I need to sell this stuff quick and get some money before I get a pull off the Old Bill.' I would give them a flash of a handful of stones wrapped in a handkerchief, mounted in beautiful settings, men's and women's, that anyone would love to wear. 'I could do you a right good deal. There was a mink coat there and a sliding cigarette case,' I'd add, 'but I don't know about them, they might be gone. Look, get them valued if you want.' Of course, I won't really let you inspect the stones, much less take them to a jeweller and if you get too close I'll go, 'What are you doing? You'll get us all nicked.' Make you feel stupid. The stress is on speed, secrecy and I'm good at it.

You're a fence, remember, I have been introduced by a friend and this is turning on your greedy switch. Of course, what I've shown you aren't real diamonds. They're jargoons – a type of zircon gemstone material. Those of us who did this con called them the jars for short and that was how the con itself got its name – 'the jars'.

If you did get close enough to the jars to test them you'd soon see they weren't the real thing. Try filing the jars and they'll mark.

Real diamonds never do. The other way to tell is to put the glass on them – there's no such thing as a flawless diamonds but these fakes are clear. But I haven't let you have a good look, have I? You're not quite sure why you haven't been able to look, though you're sure there's a good reason and if I've done very well you might even think you *have* inspected them. In the words of the old song – it's not what you do, it's the way that you do it.

I learned all my tricks from the professional conmen I met in the Queen's Road mob. I was fascinated by their game. They knew the Krays – we all knew of each other – and it was through them that I first got to hear about the twins' club, The Double R. The Krays found the venue in Bow Road, just before the old bridge near the Lea, not more than a couple of miles from the Krays' house near the bottom of Brick Lane in Bethnal Green. The family used to live just off Brick Lane at the end of Cheshire Street, though even the house has gone now. I still pass the site on the train these days when I'm travelling into London and each time I go through the area I think of how much of a change those short years made in me.

When I first visited The Double R I liked what I saw and became a regular. That was how I got to know Reggie, while Ronnie was away. Ronnie was doing a prison sentence before he eventually landed in Long Grove, the mental hospital. There were varying accounts of why he was certified – everyone seemed to have a theory. I didn't take much notice, still being busy getting to know people in the Queen's Road mob. What was happening with Ronnie didn't really make much impression on me while I was developing my technique with the jars.

Ronnie Curtis was a good example to me as I was starting out. He got the nickname 'the Prince' for always looking immaculate and for being well mannered. Albert 'the Jar' Lovett, as his nickname might suggest, was the king of our trick, though. He had built himself quite a reputation. We used to have breakfast meetings in Joe's Cafe at the top of Queen's Road in Upton Park. One sunny summer morning as we strolled out of Joe's, Ronnie suddenly spun round and slashed Albert's face to ribbons, the knife cut right through Albert's face lacerating his gums. Ronnie had discovered that Albert was having an affair with his attractive wife Sheila.

We used to get our jars through a fella named Tommy Plumley – or Red-Face Tommy. His contact in Hatton Gardens, London's jewellery district, used to supply us with the fake diamonds. Tommy was a small fella, not a tough guy, but he had a swagger that came from having all the police straight. Red-Face Tommy had money and was known for being able to bribe any of the Old Bill. At least, until I got him caught up in a chain reaction of arrests which caused such a scandal that everyone heard about it.

The risk with any of the cons we used to do was dealing all the time with strangers. On the one hand they had to be unknown for the trick to work but we knew there were grasses everywhere. Some of the fences had mates in the police – it was always useful in their line of work. They would do them a favour on occasion or they might even be a professional informer. We could hardly complain if our targets wanted to make money out of us. It came with the job. These guys wouldn't have any concern about going to the police because their fencing would be overlooked if they dropped us in it.

A mate of mine called Jim Cox, aka Coxie, got nicked in Greenwich over the jars and I was determined to straighten things out for him. Tommy was my first thought but wasn't a straightforward type you could just ask for a favour, and he didn't know me. I was just getting to know Reggie at The Double R and he was very interested in seeing how the cons worked. I think he found them quite impressive. He helped us out and with his assistance two of us had even managed to sell La Discothèque, the first disco in the West End, to an unsuspecting mug.

However, when I first asked Reggie to use his influence with Tommy, he just brushed me off with an assurance he never acted on. As the date of my friend's court case came up I became desperate and approached Reggie again. This time we both went over to Red-Face's flat above a barber shop in Hoxton. Reggie did the introductions and Red-Face asked me what it was about. I went through all the details, how my mate had got done over in Greenwich, where he was being held on remand. Tommy didn't say much but he got us to follow him downstairs, through the barber shop itself and into a toilet at the back where he kept his phone. Within minutes he was through to the policeman in charge of the case.

'My name's Tommy, I'm a little red-faced fella. You'll know who I am when you see me,' he said. 'You know that job you've got on in Greenwich? Let's meet Thursday.' With Tommy's contacts, it was that simple. The officer readily agreed to discuss the case in a pub near Guy's Hospital on the south bank of the Thames, listened to his story carefully – and nicked him. Although they gave him bail he was fuming when he came home and I thought it was best to stay out of his way. It wasn't a bad decision as things got even worse for Red-Face. He discovered that the case was based around the testimony of four drinkers standing nearby in the pub. When he was bribing the policeman they were listening to every word.

Tommy enlisted the help of the twins to recruit the same number of men, among them trusted associates such as Claude the cab driver, Larry the Lamb and Electric Les. They all made statements that they were standing nearby and they didn't hear anything. But the police had made themselves busy and revealed that the official witnesses were all doctors from Guy's who were in the pub most nights.

The case became famous, as I discovered on a Sunday, which had been shaping up to be a rather boring one until *The News of the World* came through the letterbox. I remember feeling so unmotivated that I almost couldn't be bothered to read it. They'd have to have a story about me today, I thought, to get me reading. I wasn't far wrong. I opened it up to find a spread with the headline: THE FOUR JUST MEN. There were the doctors telling their stories and I was suddenly wide awake. The feature had all the detail and the police officer who had arrested Tommy was featured in full. 'I scurfed the villain!' he was quoted as saying. 'I grabbed him by the collar and brought him to justice.' Red-Face folded and pleaded guilty – rather selfishly – as it meant his four mates went to prison alongside him for not telling the truth. They'd all gone off like a chain of fire crackers. It broke old Tommy and he died not long after that.

The jars was not the only trick I pulled. A more skilful con was 'the corner'. This involved selling nothing at all and that was always going to require more talent than was needed for the jars, when you at least had some stones to show your buyer. But what the corner and the jars did share was the necessity for an indirect approach. You had to tell your target that a mutual acquaintance asked you to have a word with them. You had something this friend said your target would be very interested in. As long as you're sure this mutual acquaintance isn't going to turn up, you're safe.

'Oh, right,' says the target. 'What's that, then?'

They might be in the market for stolen cigarettes. So that's what you say you've got a load of. It could be whisky if they aren't after snout – it can be anything you want. You haven't got it anyway, so you don't have to restrict your imagination. That was always the joke with the Queen's Road mob. If your target doesn't want what you say you're selling, find something they do want! How hard can it be? Offer them televisions. Anything. Just don't give up on them. The debates could get quite heated when we discussed customers who were being coy.

'He must want *something*!' We'd have to think hard about what would be the appropriate bait. Then we would go back to our customer and the negotiations would begin.

'How much?' asks the buyer. He's now very interested. You've been whispering your description of the goods. You want to have a bit of going back and forth on the price and the quantity because you don't want to seem too straightforward. So far, so obvious. Then comes the bit that was unique to the corner. They must come out to collect the goods, the key lies in making out that you're on the buyer's side.

'Listen, you better bring somebody with you,' you advise, 'to help you. 'Cos we might need a hand.' The idea was to lull them into a trusting state, tapping their natural greed to get them where we wanted them.

We always made sure that what we were saying didn't sound too important – it was just common sense. The buyer, we suggested, will have all this gear to take away and they will be somewhere unfamiliar. We just want to make sure they're not struggling. That's good of us, isn't it? But the real reason was to make sure they were two-handed. We could do this con anywhere, but I particularly liked to meet people at a cafe in Commercial Road, north of the Rotherhithe Tunnel. The other important part of the job was to have a friend with me.

There would be a bit of a chat at first to get everyone at their ease.

'You got the money?' I would ask.

'Yeah, got the money.'

'Show us.' One of them would reach into his coat and get out a bundle of cash. I'd gesture for him to be more discreet.

'Give it to your mate to hold,' I would say. 'We don't want no money on show round the yard. You come with me. I've got me brother-in-law there. He'll load you up.'

With that I'd leave with the buyer and we'd get in the buyer's transport and drive straight through the tunnel. Now the buyers would be split up and in completely different areas of London. We would be controlling them. That was the trick and not one you could pull now with everyone on their mobile phone.

'Pull up,' I would tell the buyer and then I would say to him, 'Hang on, I'm just going to shoot up and get the keys. I might be a couple of minutes.' With that I would disappear into a car we had previously parked out of sight nearby and leave him stranded and lost, I would then shoot back through the tunnel and park the car out of sight in another previously arranged spot.

Meanwhile, the buyer's mate would still be in the cafe. His mate might have gone but he had the money so there couldn't be anything wrong with that, could there? So on cue my partner would say, 'Taking their time, aren't they? Come on, we'll have a walk round there.' He would walk the man with the money in the opposite direction to the one I'd taken his mate, towards a pre-arranged corner.

Just before they got there I would hurriedly come round the corner and say to the mug, 'Take 100 quid out of that money, some have already been sold, the rest are loaded up and your mate's just coming now.' Having taken the money out of his pocket and with a bit of encouragement from me, I would expect him to hand me the balance. 'Your mate said he will pick you up at the café.' We would then disappear round the corner

The partner of the buyer would hang around the cafe until he began to realise that all was not well before eventually returning to the corner where we had left him and eventually going through the gates of the only nearby yard to be greeted by no lorry, no friend and a yard owner who would ask what he thought he was doing there. As reality dawned, the buyer's partner and the buyer himself would be stranded in different parts of London, left to find their way home and work out what had happened – by which time we were long gone. That was how the corner was operated and that was how it got its name. By the end of the day, everyone was round a different corner; once again it's not what you do but the way that you do it.

I got to know my way around more of London and I enjoyed the freedom, just as I liked the challenge of the mental agility involved in the corner. The travelling aspect in particular was rare at a time when most people stuck to their own area. The Krays certainly rarely strayed out of the few streets in their immediate vicinity – they moved in straight lines, more or less. I ended up with friends in places like the Elephant & Castle, over the south side of the Thames. Ronnie Curtis knew people nearby, in the Old Kent Road, and I liked their company too, drinking in pubs like the Magnet and the Bricklayers. I noticed the criminals there were more professional than many over my side of the water, though I didn't do much in the way of business with them myself.

Reggie and Ronnie hadn't even heard of any of the pubs over in South London and wouldn't have been interested in what was going on in them if they had. They were like faithful old dogs, sticking to what they knew and while they might have wanted to move on to bigger things, they were comfortable at home. That's always the killer, being comfortable, and I always felt they knew the limits of their capabilities too well, especially Reggie. But they were both too nervy to wander far.

The corner kept me busy and I built up a good idea of the kind of customer I wanted to target. Big, successful fences. All of us who did the corner avoided ordinary people unless we were really hard up and even then we'd prefer to go for someone who was just starting up as a fence. We were rarely sussed with what we called the Johnny – from Johnny Horner, corner – and we had loads of energy. Apart from veterans like Albert Lovett, we were young, fresh-faced kids and we had the enthusiasm to win anyone over – even ourselves – the really good con men end up convincing themselves on some level. They're a little bit eccentric. Tommy Hume was one veteran of the game who got himself worked up into quite an outrage when he was told a buyer wasn't going to pick up the entirely non-existent goods he'd been promised.

'You have to deliver to him,' he was told.

Tommy was fuming. 'Well, if he don't come out, he can fucking go without them!' he said in all seriousness. It was as if he'd imagined the merchandise in such detail that, in his mind, they really existed. Who could argue with that?

When customers went to the police – who overlooked their crimes or paid them for information – we were usually okay. We were good at covering our tracks and the police had no more idea than the customers who was behind the con. Some fences were more dangerous. These were the ones who had a bit of their own mob around them and they wouldn't use the police. They could be on you any time. They could see you at some later point in a pub or someone might tell them, 'I bet I know who that was.' I could deal with all that, though, and I never got caught. I was extremely cautious and I made sure I never left any traces. I was always looking out for trouble. I had a good instinct for self-preservation.

If a customer did get too close we would retreat to The Double R, where I was beginning to get on very well with Reggie. The customers didn't know that. They came crying to him and he never let on that he was on our side.

'I'll sort that out for you,' he would say, 'but don't think I'm doing it for nothing.' He got even more money out of them.

Reggie acted like a seagull following the trawler of the corner with its fishermen and swooping down to grab some of the easy pickings left behind. If it was possible for those hapless buyers to get less than nothing out of a situation, that's what they'd end up with. If Reggie did precisely nothing for them, who were they then going to complain to? In return for helping us, Reggie didn't ask for anything. He didn't even force our targets to give him anything. They just seemed to have this unshakeable belief that, whether it was us or Reggie, somehow the world owed them a living.

After Ronnie came out of prison, later on, there was an unfortunate situation when a couple of fellas who worked the con; Larry Cardy and 'Steamy' Jim, ripped off someone the twins knew.

Ronnie said, 'That money's got to go back. You can't have it.' The victim might not even have been a good friend. He could well have been someone who just offered the Krays a bigger cut to get his original money back. It was just one of those things. This target had simply got through to the twins and they wanted the money back. Sometimes that happened.

'Bring the money to me personally,' said Ronnie. This was the last thing Larry wanted to hear.

'Oh, God,' he said to me. 'I don't want to go round there.'

Jim later told me what he'd said. 'Nothing to worry about,' I said. 'Ron *loves* American comics. That's what you need to talk about. If you get him started on that you'll be safe as houses. It'll take his mind right off everything.'

Ronnie was left in complete ignorance of this conversational gambit and, as Larry should really have known, had even less idea about American comics. When Larry arrived at his home and kicked off with, 'Have you read any good comics lately?' he was lucky to get away with his life.

Later that night I saw Ronnie for a drink. Larry had at least taken the money to the Krays' place and that was probably the biggest factor counting towards his continuing existence.

'That Larry Cardy's a fucking idiot,' said Ronnie. Still not having tumbled, he remained baffled by the obsession the man seemed to have with comics.

I managed to avoid those sorts of situations most of the time. When only Reggie was around and Ronnie was still inside it was even easier. I never gave him a penny in all my life and certainly not for any of the cons. The Double R might have been a handy bolthole for us but having us there was good for Reggie too. He saw an opportunity to make a few quid now and again and more than anything else, though, he liked the con – it was brainy, it was clever and he was fascinated by it. It was him who found our very first customer, a firm in Mile End called Chambers Wood Yard.

'They'll buy a load of crooked tyres off you,' he said. 'I know who to stick up.'

Stick ups were mutual acquaintances of us and our customers and they provided the all-important initial introduction. They helped to create trust in the form of common ground. Reggie later sent other targets our way, even when he didn't get money from them himself. He knew we would be loyal to him, which we were, in those days. As the Krays were establishing themselves he was known for being fair in business and he stood out for his good manners and politeness.

Dion O'Banion, a Chicago gangster in Capone's era, was Reggie's model. The American had a florist's as one of his front

30

businesses and owning one became something of an obsession for Reggie. Nobody really knew how gangsters should behave at that time. I seized upon any nuggets of information. There wasn't the unstoppable media interest in them that there is today. Reggie didn't really have a clue how the real mob operated. Myself, I remember when *The Green Felt Jungle* made a big stir on its first publication by lifting the lid on Las Vegas gambling and Frank Sinatra. Turkus and Feder's *Murder Inc* was another rare glimpse of what went on.

The Krays went on to make their own myths. By the time their career ended there would already be almost too much being written about gangsters. Their every move was documented but what wasn't so well recorded was the way Ronnie almost ended everything way back before it had properly began.

It started with one of the cellmates he had while he was away, Bert Rossi. His nickname was Battles and he was one of the proper Italian mob living in Clerkenwell. He had been jailed for four years for the attack on Jack Spot, which had made the first newspaper story I'd read about him. Battles contacted the Kray family outside when he first realised that Ronnie was mentally ill. I'm not sure what gave it away – perhaps Ronnie had attacked Battles or he might have been getting paranoid. Either way, the family were alerted. Ronnie himself had a sentimental side and very much appreciated the gesture. He could be faithful and he never forgot.

Not long after they were both released, Battles had a falling out with some other Italians at the Central Club in Central Street in Clerkenwell. The Central was a working man's club. As a small fella, Battles asked Ronnie over, thinking that his presence might be helpful. When Ronnie arrived he was more than present – he pulled out a revolver and started shooting around the room. The place was a blur of Italians diving under tables and running for their lives. By chance Ronnie failed to hit anyone, though a bullet went through someone's jacket sleeve. Battles had no further problems with the Italians. More significantly, it was a pointer to the later shooting of George Cornell in The Blind Beggar, a demonstration that Ronnie was quite prepared to stroll in and take potshots in front of large numbers of witnesses.

Ronnie styled himself as the Colonel and life for the rest of us was undoubtedly more straightforward before his return. I don't quite remember where he was before he came out – in prison or in mental hospitals. He was certainly still ill; he went to St Clement's Mental Hospital in Mile End as a voluntary patient and he thought his dad, old Charlie, was an FBI agent for a while. Mind you, even when he didn't think that, he always hated his dad. They never got on.

Though it wasn't so apparent to begin with, Ronnie was really mad and I'm not just being judgemental here. I speak as someone who has experienced schizophrenia in my own family and I can tell you that Ronnie was even then totally insane. That's what makes me laugh when they all say how powerful he was, 'king of the underworld' and all that. It was all a charade with him. He wasn't king of anything. There was one time I remember he said to me, 'I don't care who the guv'nor is. Just so long as they don't want to be my guv'nor.' And that just about summed him up. Ronnie was always at best erratic. Despite dressing in the crispest of suits he would often as not come home with the cuffs of his shirts flapping around. He'd have given the cufflinks to a young boy somewhere.

The people who surrounded Ronnie weren't into our sort of life. I spoke the same language as the other fellas at The Double R. Ronnie's cronies didn't have the same background as us, not the ones he came out with. They wouldn't have known what you were talking about if you mentioned anything crooked. None of them had the slightest idea of what an earner was. To me they just weren't very interesting. My friendship with the twins was based around our business and that's what I was after. It could be fun but it was also work. At its best it was like being in a film – that was the excitement – and Ronnie's friends didn't quite fit into that.

At least everything was on the surface with Ronnie. He could be very urbane, whereas Reggie was much more like their father. As I got to know them both I saw that Ronnie was the more frightening, but you always felt he was genuinely pleased to see you. Reggie was buttoned up in every way. His style of speech was nervy and breathless and with his suit done up tight he would be in constant movement even while he was talking to you, twitching and rocking around on the balls of his feet as if he were in the ring waiting for the round to start. Very serious. Both of them were naturally suspicious and Reggie always looked quizzical, one eyebrow raised as if it was doing it on its own, as if he was betraying the fact that he didn't quite believe what you were saying, whatever you might be talking about. He always wanted to know who you'd seen, who was about, I understood this and it didn't bother me but it worried most people.

The difference was that Reggie didn't have the same kind of mental health problems to begin with. His problem was more some kind of deep-seated personality disorder and over time that became more apparent. Towards the end of their reign, Reggie's own madness came to the fore. There would be much less to tell between the twins by then. Alcohol played a massive part. The twins virtually merged into one mass of drunken rage. But in the early days Reggie had the facade of the charming, rough-edged club owner.

I thought it was best to be scared of both and I was hard to frighten. Each was as strong as an ox and although I would be critical of them, I wouldn't question their reputation. Others have, over the years, and it's true they did go into a decline, but there was a time when you could go into a pub and everyone would be in awe of this double vision they presented. They were always together and, usually, united. The rumour was they were no good on their own. The point was, they were never on their own. What chance did you have?

The twins had their own agenda which they never shared with anyone else. They would always get the first blow in. That terrified everyone more than anything else. You never knew when they were going to attack until it was too late. That was how they operated.

There were always fights in The Double R. That was largely down to the licensing laws being different the other side of the old Bow Bridge, east of Mile End. It was the border of London proper, really, and if you headed west from the Stratford and Canning Town side after 10.30 pm you could drink at The Double R in Bow Road for an extra half hour. It was also the local place that served alcohol in the afternoons, a fact that was not lost on the Thames dockers. They used to plague us – they'd 'bomp on', which I think meant they'd turn up at the dockyard, sign in and then say there wasn't a boat for them to work on. They'd then go in search of drink. But The Double R kept its licence by being a strictly members-only club. The doormen adhered to the regulations, taking down names and addresses in a book. There was no choice. When the police staged one of their occasional raids on the place they would corral all the punters and check them off against the recorded details.

Without fail at least one docker would kick off, having to leave their name when they should have been working.

'I ain't signing no fucking book. I only want a fucking drink.'

It makes me laugh to think about it now – it was always the same and whoever did it would always get knocked out by the doorman. Big Tommy Brown AKA The Bear and an ex-heavyweight fighter and Billy Donovan, a local tough guy who was very handy with a cosh. Dockers were an entirely separate breed. Huge men armed with the fearsome hooks they used on the docks and they wouldn't even see Reggie with his suit, his collar and his tie. And the sight of the doormen didn't put them off either. Though you'd think they would back off a little bit when they saw big Pat Connolly behind the counter. Pat was the barman rather than a bouncer, but he was 28 stone – largely fat – and covered in scars. When he started swearing at you in his thick Scottish accent you knew you were dealing with a proper Glaswegian. And if you had any sense you would be properly terrified. The dockers weren't. They always used to have a go though and they'd always be taken out. But even Pat was nervous around Ronnie Kray and no more so than the night Ronnie came in from the rain.

Ronnie didn't have far to travel from home to his club but it was chucking it down that night and it would have been sensible to take a cab. But not Ronnie. He was just thinking to himself, Oh, this is nice. He walked all the way in his immaculate, trademark three-piece suit, the rain streaming through his hair and down his face. He must have felt as if he was in the shower. I was in the club when he made his entrance. Everyone could see the evidence of his madness as he strode damply up to the counter.

'I'll have a gin and bitter lemon, please,' he said to big Pat.

The barman was terrified in the way that people often are when they see someone so completely divorced from reality. Pat could be difficult to understand when he was in full Glaswegian flow but now he carefully articulated each word as if his life depended on it. His hands shook slightly as he poured out the gin and he looked over to Ronnie who was staring straight ahead – soaked through, steaming. Pat was nervous about getting the order even slightly wrong.

'Do you want...would you like...a *bitter* lemon...or a *bit of* lemon?'

Chapter Three

AT HOME WITH THE KRAYS

The Krays were often embarrassingly strapped for cash. We made a lot of money when we were based out of The Double R. But none of us saved any of it. There was no cheque book or bank account for us. It was just a case of getting the money, stuffing it in your pocket and going out for the night. We all looked the part. Taking our cue from the twins, we had the suits, we had the cars and we were all very confident. It helped to convince the victims of my cons that I was successful at business. But there was no substance behind anything we did and that was sometimes humiliatingly obvious.

I saw it when we were all out in the West End one night. Back then you could order a big bottle of spirits and save what you didn't use. You would go through half a bottle or so, the waiter came to measure how much had been consumed and when you paid he would put your name on the bottle. You'd get to finish it next time you were in. Reggie was so hard up at a nightclub owned by Danny La Rue that he discreetly poured some tonic in a bottle of gin to make it look like he hadn't had that much. The waiters had torches so they could see the level of remaining alcohol in the dark surroundings of the club. Our man that night was startled to see what looked like tiny fish in the bottle – Reggie had poured in bitter lemon by mistake. That was how impoverished the twins were at any one time. Famous, feared, but potless.

They were just all about the publicity and being known, making sure they were seen at the right places, even if they couldn't quite afford them. The Society, which later became Tramp, became the favoured spot for the firm. Apparently the Jermyn Street spot was frequented by Princess Margaret, which would have been more impressive were it not for the fact that it was rarer to find a London club she *hadn't* visited. You imagined she'd feel at home, though. This was dining in the grand style, an experience lit by extravagant chandeliers. Far from the regular haunts. Into this elegant world came the Krays, ten-handed with Ronnie. His men always watched their boss order his favourite, double spaghetti bolognese for himself and without fail each of them asked for the same. This wasn't because they were frightened of him – Ronnie was paying the bill. It was their work's treat and only those who were in favour would be asked. You had to go and you had to make sure you didn't spend more than him. A fella called Dukey Osbourne was there one night, another of the loyal mob, and raised the tone still further when wandering violinist 'Gypsy' Adams, who made his way from table to table, got within earshot. 'Gyp! Gyp!' said Dukey loudly, pausing over his spaghetti to wave a pound note he wanted to offer in return for some personal choice of tune. It's safe to assume Princess Margaret didn't do the same on her visit.

The West End wasn't where we would normally start our evenings, though. It was more usually in The Double R. With the name of the Krays attached, it was the place to be. The legendary Jack Spot once came in the club with a friend. Johnny Carter was a fellow gangster whose leg, in an incident more reminiscent of Monty Python than criminal activity, South Londoner Frankie Fraser was said to have tried to saw off. I have no idea if it was true, though I did know that Carter was definitely a tough guy and he came from a mob based over the Elephant & Castle. As a younger man coming up myself, I paid quite a bit of attention to these myths and legends. I could see how handy it was to have a good story.

The regular crowd in The Double R were a tight circle of friends. We all started off just as the Krays themselves were beginning to find success. We were the nucleus of the club itself – Georgie 'Ossie' Osbourne, Dukey Osbourne, Johnny Squib, Dickie Moughton, Billy Donovan, big Pat Connolly, Tommy Brown and Dicky Morgan. Pat was intelligent and a bit warm, shrewd. The rest of them were loyal but over time the group fell apart as the twins became more erratic and it had disastrous consequences for Ossie.

The twins introduced him to La Monde, a smart drinking club in the World's End area of the King's Road in Chelsea. Ossie became close to the owner, Jamette – a very evil woman – and eventually shared her flat above the club. Jamette had emboldened the twins after telling Ronnie that the then commissioner of the Met, Sir Joseph Simpson, was a closet masochist who she would regularly whip and abuse to order and she assured them she could handle him. This same woman was the one who, when Reggie chinned Bimbo Smith knocking his false teeth out, stamped on them, and on her daughter's 16th birthday asked Ronnie to deflower her. Ronnie duly obliged.

One evening Ossie didn't feel like coming down to play host to Ronnie and his party and Ronnie went berserk. He ripped the club apart, tearing the decor off the walls and trashing the furniture. Ossie never seemed to get over the shock of Ronnie's reaction and died from a heart attack not long after.

But the notoriety of the Krays' name ensured that despite their behaviour, more people joined the group – what became the firm – and eventually it got too unwieldy. It was the sheer number of hangers-on and celebrity spotters that would prove to be the undoing for the Krays. It was ironic in a way – we were much tighter in the early days and we were at our best long before anyone had thought of calling the Krays a 'firm'.

In those early years, there were a few among us who liked to go out during the day and a popular destination for them was The Spieler, a gambling house in Wellington Way, almost opposite The Double R. It wasn't for me. I never used to gamble. Didn't know how, didn't want to know. I'd had a go once when I was 15 and I lost all my factory wages. But The Spieler was popular enough; it was next door to a police yard and it eventually got raided but it was somewhere you could go for a cup of tea and where you might arrange to see people over The Double R later in the evening.

I preferred The Double R itself and when that closed we headed to the West End for a big night out. Everything revolved around drinking back then. We socialised together but that's also how most of our business was done. I didn't know anyone who didn't drink – there would have been something suspicious about someone who didn't. Everything was done in a bit of a soft haze. And I knew all the best clubs in the '60s. I loved them and in the West End they were far less male dominated than The Double R. The nightclub hostesses formed a major part of the attraction of the times and, besides, it was different at The Double R once the Colonel had come home. The Krays' place wasn't somewhere you'd go out with a girlfriend or with the wife. You had to be on your guard and know who Ronnie Kray was speaking to and who was out of bounds. There was one bloke who we were told to ignore one night – a reporter for *The Sunday People* called Tom Bryant. His crime was to file a nasty piece about a friend of Ronnie's called Frank Mitchell. He called him 'the mad axeman'.

'We're having nothing to do with him,' said Ronnie. 'He's been coming in here and we've been right friendly with him and now he's wrote that piece in the paper.'

I don't even recall if I saw the offending article but I wouldn't forget being told to blank him. Mitchell had escaped from Broadmoor and found a house with an old couple. He told them to behave themselves and picked up an axe by way of suggesting what might happen if they didn't. Bryant gave him the nickname, which stayed with him for the rest of his life. Ronnie ignoring Bryant was all part of the big boss image he liked to project.

I remember where I first ran into Ronnie. Behind Mile End Station there used to be a billiard hall. There was a cinders pitch, an area of paving between the two buildings, and I was heading across the cinders to the hall to speak to Reggie. I saw him – or I thought I saw him – near the hall.

'Reg!' I called out. He turned around slowly and replied with the nasal sneer that was often in his voice.

'I think you want my brother.' There was something unnerving about his measured, deliberate delivery and the way he looked at me. He'd just come home at that point. One trouser leg was shorter than the other and you could see a hole in his sock. He wasn't alone, though I don't remember who it was who accompanied him. I do know that he went away again not long after that.

Eventually Ronnie returned for good and settled back into life in the area and I inevitably got to know him as a result of being good friends with Reggie. The twins were often as not both at their family home, 178 Vallance Road, off Whitechapel Road and between Brick Lane and The Double R. It was a small house and they used the front rooms both upstairs and downstairs for receiving visitors.

There was a short hallway from the downstairs front room to a small kitchen with a table, which made it the dining room as well. Next to that was a scullery space of the type where a family might drag in the tin bath. Straight people were never invited, though even those who had just got out of prison and had come to pay their respects to the twins were received with utter contempt. The Krays had no time for them, dismissing them as 'jailbirds'. They had little time for anyone, to be honest.

New faces were given an initiation of sorts by the caged mynah bird lurking in a corner of the kitchen. 'What's your name!' it said, sounding like Ronnie himself, rather whiny and nasal. Reflecting the main concern of the household it could also say, 'Some money! Get some money!' as well as 'Mum! Maaahhhhm!' As an encore it could do old Charlie senior's hacking cough and a passable version of the trains rumbling by on the viaduct up the road.

Guests in the kitchen were perched on a chair with their back to the bird and it sometimes took advantage of those who hadn't noticed it. But the twins hadn't bought the bird deliberately to give people a shock. Most visitors were nervous enough just being in the presence of the Krays and would leap up in terror when it chipped in loudly with its choice phrases – 'What's your name?' causing particular panic.

I spent many hours in that house and got to observe the twins at close quarters. They were never really off duty but when they were relaxed, Reggie – the more stable of the two, at least in those days – demonstrated no sense of humour whatsoever. Ronnie never stopped laughing. Even when a mate bought over a copy of *Private Eye* that lampooned the pair of them. I'd been reading the satirical magazine since it came out and was a fan of Richard Ingrams but neither of the twins had the faintest idea what *The Eye* was about. Among its other achievements, it was the first publication to feature the Krays. The piece that Ronnie saw was written very much in the style of the twins and made merciless fun of them. Ronnie howled with laughter and it kept him amused all day. All his visitors had to read it and he long referred to himself as a 'well-known thug and poof' in general company. Reggie forced a smile but you could tell he just didn't get it. *Private Eye*'s interest in the twins later helped to popularise the idea that they were somehow cool and part of the

Swinging Sixties, but that was very wide of the mark. They were always apart.

The twins themselves were not into popular culture, even as they were becoming part of it. It may well have been the piece in *The Eye* that caused the Oxford Student Union to have a close escape when they invited the twins to take part in a debate, the subject, 'Is the law an ass?'. The twins were terrified at the thought of it and the invite was kept a closely guarded secret amongst a select few. I shudder to think of their reaction when some young intellectual would have undoubtedly had them tongue tied and floundering. I was unusual in their crowd for liking all sorts of comedy, not just *The Eye*, and I loved French gangster movies. Still do. *Classe tous Risques* (*Consider All Risks*) is a favourite; a 1960 film with Lino Ventura and Jean-Paul Belmondo. Another Ventura classic was *The Second Breath – Le Deuxième Souffle*. It was more recently remade, but it wasn't as good as the black-and-white original. Sometimes you shouldn't go back. The twins didn't go to the pictures at all but I think Ronnie would have liked *Repo Man*, the Alex Cox film from the 1980s. Harry Dean Stanton is in his car when he looks around and says, 'Ordinary people. I fucking hate them!' It's still one of my favourite lines in any movie.

Ronnie said something similar about the straight world when were sitting in a car outside a pub in Bow; he was looking to stick it on someone or other and he was feeling particularly full of bitter hatred. He was rather less elegant in his description than Stanton as he gazed at his fellow drinkers.

'Look at them. Fucking hate them,' he said. 'I'd like to hold them down and let a black man fuck them.'

Both brothers really did despise almost everyone – straight and criminal. It was just the world of the middle and upper classes that both brothers respected. They always hoped they would be able to join them some day. But that wasn't the same as liking. That was wanting something they'd never had. They were generally just very antisocial and dismissive of anyone they couldn't use. The best you could hope for was to be accepted – and that applied to me as much as anyone else. It was all just business.

They dressed to reflect their aspirations and to show how far they'd come. When they were young the family business had been clothes buying, but it was all second-hand. As kids they would go cold calling with a bag to ask for unwanted old clothes, though they would take any old gold and more or less any old anything. Once home, they cleaned and pressed the clothes and then I guess they sold them on. By the time I knew them they could splash out on anything they wanted and their taste was another way to tell them apart. Ronnie wore a Savile Row suit and crocodile shoes whereas Reggie was strictly East End, his suit from Woods the Tailor on Kingsland Road. If Reggie was an East End boy then Ronnie was a West End girl.

It was usually open house at Vallance Road, as long as you were respectful to everyone and everything there – that was what it was all about. You had to match their style too. They were surprisingly prim and they'd never mention bodily functions in conversation. On the surface their place was a model of suburban respectability, tidy and a bit severe. But only in appearance. The twins' mother, Violet, often written about as the Queen Mum of the East End, set the tone. I would often meet with the twins in Pellicci's, the cafe at the top of their road – it's still there. One day we had a cup of tea before heading back to Vallance Road where she opened the door.

'Did you see that fella, Reg?' she said. 'I sent him down the cafe to see ya.'

'Yeah,' said Charlie. 'Reggie nutted him.'

'I thought he would,' she said.

Reggie himself added, 'He was a fucking nuisance.'

Family dinners were no safer. Not even the day Ronnie, kitted out with pressed trousers and braces, was enjoying a big, steaming bowl of chunky stew. An English bull terrier dozed by his feet. Dukey Osbourne was also there. I could hear old Charlie's tread in the corridor outside and Ronnie squawked like his mynah bird, 'Maaahmm! Maaahhhhm!' He hated his father. 'It's the old bastard!'

Like his sons, old Charlie always wore a nice suit – particularly when he was out drinking, which was quite a lot of the time. Setting great store by his ability to clean and press clothes, he claimed he could get all the blood out of his sons' outfits after they had been fighting. He staggered through the door, adjusting his tie and his cuffs. Ronnie continued with his baiting.

'He's here, Mum! Rotten, drunken old cunt!' Violet was working in the kitchen and although she must have heard the complaints, she didn't respond.

Charlie sneered. 'What I've heard about you today, son. Well, I never. Can't believe it,' he said. 'You're gone! You're gone!'

Ronnie's eyes had become fixed, staring. His hands gripped his knife and fork very hard. Without turning, he slid his eyes around to gaze at his father as his whole head shook with rage.

Charlie continued. 'What they've told me about you today down The 99 (a pub in Bishopsgate). Oh. You make me feel sick, it's disgusting.' Charlie had discovered his son was gay. He might not be able to say the word 'homosexual' but that was what he meant and Ronnie knew it.

'Shut up!' growled Ronnie.

'Shut up? You're fucking gone, you are!'

At this, Ronnie jumped up, startling the dog, and took a couple of paces across the room to face his father, knife and fork in his hands. I sat at the table, not looking at Dukey, dying a death and just listening as Ronnie repeatedly shouted 'Shut up!' into his father's face. The terrier joined the family bust-up, trotting across the room and biting the old boy on the leg. Ronnie had his knife in one big fist, raised above his father. He held himself back, though the knife grazed one cheek. It was enough.

'You cut me, son!' shouted his father. 'Oh, what have you come to?' Looking over Ronnie's shoulder he called into the kitchen, 'Violet! He's cut me! Oh, my God!'

I took the opportunity to make a discreet exit – I don't know what happened to Dukey on that day – and Charlie's drunken shouts faded as I moved quietly and fast down the passageway and out the front door. That was that afternoon's cabaret concluded as far as I was concerned.

The next day I called round the house for Reggie. He came out limping slightly and grimacing.

'What's the matter, Reg? I said.

'The Colonel's kicked me up the bollocks,' he answered. I didn't ask why.

But visiting them was mainly a social thing. You had to do it but you didn't get much business done, even when they weren't at each other's throats. It was understood that when you went over to see them there, or to some degree at The Double R, you were on call, if only to keep them company. Sometimes I would go over when I had a scheme of my own or made a few quid and we'd go for a drink together. But at the same time I never worked for them, as such. Nobody did, really. The job was always to work out how to make money out of the situations in which the twins put me. They never gave anybody anything. At least, not in financial terms. I did get a couple of presents. One was a monkey, in a cage, the other – continuing the animal theme – was a Great Dane. It was rare enough that Reggie willingly gave anything anyway.

On those occasions when business was discussed, it often included a trip to the local bathhouse – back then public baths were still very popular. The entrance fee included a towel and you locked yourself in one of the little baths and they'd see to it that you sweated nicely. 'More hot in number seven!' and similar cries could be heard all the time. 'More cold in number three!' Staff charged up and down the corridor making sure that everyone was happy. It was very relaxing and a favourite destination for the Krays and an entourage, which regularly occupied the whole of the local baths. The experience was enhanced by various fads. For one, Tommy Brown advocated splashing surgical spirit all over the body, for some reason now lost in time. You never asked for the reasoning behind these brilliant suggestions. There probably wasn't any. It was some kind of toughening process and it was certainly that as the baths resounded to the agonised yells of those of us who had spilt spirit on our bollocks.

If you had a proposition to put to the twins, or a shop or other business you wanted them to back, you knew you were doing well if they invited you to join them in that day's excursion. It was informal and light-hearted, yet it was an important ritual for those in their circle. People who didn't know them that well were startled when Reggie announced, 'We're going over the baths.' His audience would look as if it was the most normal thing in the world.

'You want to come over and have a bath?'

'Oh, yeah, yeah. Baths? Good idea.'

As one man, everyone in the house – anything from six to ten, or even more – would up and troop across over the street to the nearest bath. We marched across in crocodile formation like something out of *Reservoir Dogs* and it must have been quite a sight. Naturally, as part of the Krays, we went to the head of the queue each time.

Harry was the man who ran the baths and he later opened the gym above The Double R. On his suggestion the twins installed a couple of sunbeds and it was them who first gave them a go. But they didn't wear the protective goggles and both ended up blinder than usual for a few days with a nasty case of conjunctivitis. They got some funny stares, both looking as if they'd been crying their eyes out.

When outsiders came to Vallance Road, local businessmen chasing opportunities with the Krays, they were mainly very naive. You'd have to be to go there in the first place. It wasn't as if the Krays controlled the area so tightly that you couldn't start a legitimate company without them. But there were those who seemed to want them on board and that was probably far more dangerous. Some hopefuls were after finance or a bit of advice but the twins were essentially clueless when it came to anything except clubs. Clubs were different – that was their world and Reggie and Charlie in particular worked well in it, though even there they had their limitations.

Photographer David Bailey tried to take over a club with Reggie in Stratford Place near Oxford Street. I thought it was a brilliant suggestion but Reggie was strangely unenthusiastic and I just couldn't move him. When there was no audience I could usually talk sense to him and when he came up with all sorts of unlikely excuses I guessed the real reason. He didn't have his whack to put in – he had no money. The famous David Bailey might want to be seen with the famous Reggie Kray but he wanted his money even more. That was very typical. The celebrities I met through the Krays were shrewder at business than those of us who had less money and needed to be more careful.

As I didn't earn a wage myself I had the use of the Krays franchise to my own advantage. Their name could be useful enough on its own sometimes, as a friend of mine Harry Abrahams discovered when we were walking through Soho and he decided he wanted to go in what he thought was a strip club. As I immediately realised, it was a rip-off – a clip joint. There was a bird on the door who played on his enthusiasm and, despite being convinced that disaster lay before us, I eventually agreed. The girl tried to get Harry to buy soft drinks, promising him that she would meet him around the corner. It was the classic con, but he was mesmerised.

The club was run by a Scotsman who came up when he heard me arguing with the girl. I was getting really annoyed and the owner could tell that something was going to go off if he wasn't careful. On home turf, he thought, he started to get aggressive and I said, 'Oh, for fuck's sake. I'm with the Krays.' He looked terrified. Of course, I could have been lying for all he knew but maybe there was just something about the way I carried myself. You would have to be sure of yourself to pretend you knew the twins if you didn't – just in case the person you were talking to knew them for real. The owner started apologising; we were offered drinks and everything changed. That was how it was – everyday reality at the height of the Krays' fame.

The twins had a reputation for making a lot of their money from protection rackets, but although this was a favourite scare story for newspapers, it was completely untrue. It just didn't work like that for them, not in Soho and certainly not in our neighbourhood. You can't go around demanding half someone's takings with menaces. In the end straight businesses go to the police. You couldn't keep that up. The exception was if there was a fellow criminal of theirs who'd had a good result, they knew he had money and couldn't go to the Old Bill – that would be the protection racket, if you could call it that. That was about as business-like as they got.

Their real mission, if you could call it that, was to cull the old-school gangsters. They made themselves known by fighting their way up the ranks and that was at least as important as having regular income. Reggie was the more diligent. He was always at work from the moment he woke up to last thing at night – and his work often consisted of chinning people. He would go out specifically to invite older villains back to the club and then he'd do them. He made sure that Ronnie knew all about how many more people he'd clumped than his brother.

'What were you doing last night?' he asked. 'Cos I was working until one o'clock this morning. I chinned so-and-so.'

And so it would go on. It was a way of marking out territory. There was a spate of this from Reggie. He was doing it ever such a lot. He got the taste for it – I'd say he was addicted, perfecting his left hook.

Ronnie was far less devious in many ways. You wouldn't get a sly right-hander off him. Or a left hook. That said, he might kill you – but you wouldn't be tormented. Mostly, Ronnie was more likely to ignore you. He was often just confused – and this was his mental illness coming out. There was the time a couple were ordering at the other end of the counter in Esmeralda's Barn one night and Ronnie muttered, 'Look at him. It's one of that Canning Town mob.' I didn't comment – I'd never seen the fella before. Ronnie started to do a contemptuous nasal imitation of the Canning Town accent – our part of London was so tribal that there were real differences between them and Ronnie's neighbourhood, which wasn't really that far away in Bethnal Green. The object of Ronnie's scorn soon realised he was being watched and came over. I later found out he was actually from Fulham – not that it would have done any good to try and convince Ronnie of that – and he was perfectly polite.

'Can I buy you a drink, Ron?'

'Yeah,' said Ronnie flatly. 'But I am with some people.'

'That's all right. I'm buying.'

Ronnie bought everyone in the club a drink.

The man was panicked. 'Ron, I'm sorry, I didn't realise. I haven't got the money.'

A fella called Dougie King was the doorman at the club.

'Mr King,' called Ronnie. 'Would you come over here please and escort this gentleman from the premises?'

He carried on with his evening as if nothing had happened – Reggie would never have had the humour to do that. It was this dryness which offset the unpredictability in Ronnie's character. If you were wise you took him at face value and he could seem all the funnier for the sense of relief you felt that everything was okay – for the moment. The best moments for me came when he went off at some bizarre tangent while I was around to hear it but not the focus. Like when we were riding in his car with a club owner called Steff. He was up front with Steff and me and Coxie were in the back.

'Could you find me a Chinese houseboy?' asked Ronnie, in full Colonel mode. He was deadly serious. If it was anybody else you would ask, 'Why?', but not with Ronnie. Coxie and I held in our laughter until we were dropped off at Mile End Station, grateful to have an excuse to get away. We ran down the stairs and collapsed onto the platform in hysterics, thinking of how somewhere above us Steff was no doubt trying to hold a sensible conversation and fend off Ronnie. He did have a flair about him – he was stylish, really.

Reggie lacked the humour but he made up for it with his business schemes. He always had something going on with the local car dealers. Most of them in Mile End were at what was called the zump. This involved tracking down cars that had something wrong with them. The dealer buys cheap cars that, apart from the fault, would have been quite nice according to the official price guides. Then one of the Krays would find a likely customer to front up, just an ordinary person, offer them a car virtually for free. All they had to do was agree to sign for it. The dealers got the finance at the list price, the customers signed for it – and got a few quid for their trouble – and the finance company would then find that the customer didn't pay off what he owed. Occasionally a car dealer would be arrested but mostly it was a nice racket.

Reggie always had a good car out of it and he never paid a penny for any of them. The first one I remember him having was a bottle green Mercedes 220SE Coupé. I'm not much of a car person but it looked amazing. Then there was the big American car, his Ford Fairlane. You'd see him gliding up and down Mile End Road like something out of a film. It was fun, actually. In the end, that was what we were doing this for – a good time.

Ronnie did have a go at driving himself, once. He got one of the dealers to get him a Jaguar Mark IX, a dignified motor not unlike a Rolls Royce. Beautiful. Having not passed a test, he left the insuring of the car to one of the brothers. One day in The Spieler he fancied a drive, got in the car and went straight into a lamp post.

When a policeman soon arrived on the scene, Ronnie said, 'Here, don't worry about that,' and gave him a fiver. It was a typical Ronnie gesture. But the uniformed police and CID were totally different. You couldn't bribe a PC at that time – the CID nicknamed them 'wooden tops' – and in any case, not all police were corrupt by any means. The gangs I knew often had insiders working for them on the force but you couldn't guarantee that and even the most bent of officers would not simply take money from complete strangers. Ronnie must have realised that they always had to know who they were dealing with – always. He would have had to have a name to mention at least – and even then they'd probably only talk to the face they knew. I've never personally given a policeman a penny. Ronnie was just trying it on.

He was duly charged with both driving without a licence and bribing a policeman. At the station they asked him for his profession and on the spur of the moment he said he bred dogs. The local newspaper ran with: LOCAL DOG BREEDER CHARGED WITH BRIBERY.

Reggie had more success with the car dealers than in debt collecting. He tried collecting for a while and returned from one mission saying that it was the worst game in the world. He learned his lesson after getting involved with a fella called Danny Shay, who was a sort of long firm operator – a fraudster – working in his own circle in Hampstead. A Jewish businessman named Maurice Podro was being slow in settling his invoices. To my way of thinking, this was just his working method. Some people just don't pay until the last minute – it's sharp and mean but that's how commerce works in general, in my experience.

The tone of the disagreement was set when Danny took a swipe at his opponent's chest with an umbrella while Reggie brought Ossie along. But Maurice Podro went to the police and Reggie and Ossie got 18 months each. Having served a third he was out for another six months before losing his appeal and having to go back to serve the rest. It was back in jail that he met Frank Mitchell, a big giant of a man, who would later cause the twins a lot of problems when they came up with the idea of breaking him out of prison. The sentence put Reggie off debt collecting and it underlined the reason that the twins avoided getting into protection – the risk of someone going to the police was just too great.

With Reggie out of the way, Ronnie came up with a number of ideas while he was solely in charge. One idea was to use carrier pigeons to collect protection money – but that was as detailed as the proposition went. Another was to open a brothel on the Thames. A floating brothel on a barge. The reasoning behind this was no less obscure. When Ronnie came up with schemes like this, it was usually best not to get deeply involved. My response was generally just to agree with him, even when he asked me if I would be in charge of the wine cellar. It was one of the scattiest

49

proposals I'd ever heard, not least because I was drinking like a fish at the time and was the last person you'd want in charge of the alcohol. Inevitably, Ronnie had forgotten the whole thing by the next morning. We were all relieved when Reggie got out.

Life around the twins was as chaotic as it sounds. There were no strict regulations you could follow. It was really all about how they felt on a particular day and whether someone's behaviour threatened their largely selfish interests. A fella named Ronnie Marwood became a *cause célèbre* after he stabbed a policeman with a diver's knife and killed him. He came from North London and the dancehall where the attack happened was around his way in Highbury. We all had to have an opinion about what he'd done and what people were saying about it. The twins were obsessed. But you had to be careful that you expressed the right opinion. It went without saying that you backed Marwood over the police and it would be a very unwise customer at The Double R who would say anything else. This was another example of the tense, peculiar atmosphere in the place. Everything was significant and you could never drop your guard. It was the embodiment of that old saying, a still tongue keeps a wise head. Always good to remember around the twins but not so easy for some people to do once they had a few of an evening.

Ronnie was a friend of the Nashes, another mob we knew. Jimmy Nash was practically one of us. You could see him most days in The Spieler. The Nashes had a row in The Pen Club, an illegal drinking den in Spitalfields. A fella there belted one of them and the Nashes went up there to sort him out. They ended up going up against the owners of the club, bank robbers who themselves had only just come home from long-term sentences in Dartmoor. Jimmy Nash shot one of them in the head and killed him and shot another – Billy Ambrose – in the stomach. That was enough to get Jimmy arrested and it looked like enough to get him hanged. But then someone gave evidence to the contrary and the case collapsed, probably not least because one of those who had been there that night with the Nashes had a father who was a policeman. That all got a bit murky and we probably don't want to delve into that too much. But for a while Jimmy Nash was another one about who you just had to have an opinion – the right one.

The twins' reactions were frequently unpredictable. I remember a fella called Eric Mason had a little club in the West End and I got on well with him. He didn't look like a tough guy, but he had done loads of time, including being on the quarry party down in Dartmoor. He was famous for having an erratic temper but I never saw that side of him myself. Then there was Frankie Fraser from South London, by contrast, a legend and a real rabble rouser. Even in prison he'd be trying to organise riots and he never did anything alone. He and Eric had an argument one night in The Astor Club and when they went outside for a fight, Fraser had a whole mob with him. Eric was attacked with an axe and when he instinctively put his hand up to protect himself, the axe went right through it and into his head.

I sent someone to the hospital to find out what had happened.

He said, 'They said, "Where do you wanna be dumped? Around Vallance Road?"'

This was a mortal insult, another way of sarcastically asking if someone you've just injured wants to go to see his friends. I saw it as a quite a challenge and I was surprised when the twins didn't want to do anything about it. This was one occasion when they didn't want to have an opinion about what had happened.

When the twins did fight, I never saw anybody ever throw a punch back. Not one person in all the years I knew them. The reason was simple and it was one of the many things I learned from them. They always took people by surprise. Nobody ever had a chance. Reggie, with his greater reserves of patience and guile, could even wait a day or two. Ronnie was something else entirely. He would be much more likely just to charge in there. And he always had a fantasy about having the fight to end all fights. He imagined himself placing a photograph next to his heart in his chest pocket, a picture of a boy he met on a trip to Tangier, whose name he had long forgotten. Ronnie would take a gun up high on a roof, in this daydream. In reality he was no marksman, but he thought of himself having a shoot-out with whoever he felt was the biggest threat at the time.

In more rational moments, both Reggie and, to a lesser extent, Ronnie realised that they would need help to be able to move up to the next level, whatever that turned out to be. They recruited new people to refresh the cause and, although these characters were

51

never officially announced, I could always tell their importance by the way that the twins got more excited and nervous. The buzz going around the local pub was a giveaway. One night, when everyone had their best clean collar and tie on, I knew there was going to be an interesting arrival.

Me and Georgie Osbourne, in particular, were very intrigued by the mystery the twins were creating about our guest. It was a financial adviser named Leslie Payne. He was tall, well spoken and very smart. We started calling him George Saunders after the famous actor of the time. He was very much the smoothie businessman, but a conman too – not the street sort, but something more sophisticated.

'Do you know, I could live on £30 a week?' he said that first night. Back then £30 was about twice what most people earned and a typically snotty comment from him. We didn't end up taking him very seriously, but the twins did. Very much so. He was going to be a front man for them; he was going to take them places. Leslie was going to help them take the next step up the ladder. They employed him to stretch themselves.

Payne told them about a new town being built in the north of Nigeria. With the right amount of money behind him he could be a part of a scheme which included Ernest, son of Labour's Lord Manny Shinwell. Ernest himself was at Vallance Road one day at the same time as Freddy Bird, an old Mile End face who knew the twins from way back – old school failure, like so many of them around the twins. His task was to give Shinwell a lift to his next engagement in Surrey. I was curious about how the former public schoolboy and Freddy would get on and later asked him.

'He said he's got a chicken farm down there,' said Freddy, 'and I said to him, "Oh, do you? I breed chickens also." So he said, "Which breed?" I said, "Red ones." He was very impressed. He said, "I do like to have a sensible conversation."'

Fired up by the Nigerian plan, Ronnie, Charlie and Leslie Payne went out to see Enugu, the new town, for themselves. They were, as always, very secretive about finances but drew money from somewhere before they left. They also raised the necessary investment, which I did know about because I knew the people they talked to. It was the experience of travelling itself which was fantastic for Ronnie, someone who spent so much time close to home. And yet his interests remained much the same, even away on the trip.

'Is there anything you'd like to see?' his hosts asked.

'Yeah,' he said. 'Would you show me around the local prison?'

He was given a tour of the facilities as a visiting dignitary. Ronnie returned from the trip with Charlie, the financial adviser and his souvenir big knife. But something went wrong out there on a subsequent trip. The money didn't get to where it should have been – I never knew the details – but the upshot was that his brother Charlie and Payne later ended up as inmates of the Nigerian nick.

Back home, Reggie was left to run around like a headless version of one of Freddy Bird's 'red' chickens, frantically raising more money to get his brother out. I accompanied him on one of the fundraisers. We paid a visit to some car dealer's house one night.

'Reg, Reg,' said the fella, 'I'm having a row with the wife. Can I speak to you another time?'

'You're bothering me with your domestic squabbles while my brother's in the nick in Nigeria!'

He grabbed the dealer by the throat and slammed him up against the door, starting to strangle him. Amid the choking and shouting, a small Scotty dog ran out of the house and attached itself to Reggie's leg, yapping bravely. It was closely followed by the man's wife, who added her piercing scream to the general confusion. Somehow we extracted Reggie and somehow he managed to assemble enough money in the end to get Charlie home.

The scheme itself didn't come to anything, but it was a relief just to have Ronnie out of the country for a while. It was the same whenever the Krays were abroad. They went to Jersey and thinking back now I can remember only the intense sense of being able to relax and breathe easily for a while. It was as if I was having a holiday at the same time. Ronnie also went to Ibiza, having become enthused after hearing good reports from a friend. He was in The Double R that same night.

'So you didn't go?'

'I been,' he said. 'I didn't like it.'

'What's wrong with it?' I asked.

'It's not what I thought it was,' he said. 'It's different.'

The speed of his trip was soon explained. Having got off the plane and as far as the airport building, Ronnie decided there and then that Ibiza was not for him. He didn't even leave the airport and got the next plane back.

Chapter Four

Shooting George Dixon

I didn't know either of the two men Ronnie was attacking in The Double R. One minute he had been talking to me and the next he was steaming into them. Until that point it had been a very quiet night in the club. At that time they were running a gym above it and Ronnie and I had been standing downstairs. I had my back to the door but he had an uninterrupted view of the whole place. We weren't talking about anything particularly important when Ronnie suddenly broke off.

He said, 'Excuse me a minute, Mick.'

Ronnie walked around me and all the way along the largely deserted bar. That was when he laid into one of the strangers, seemingly without any provocation. He was punching him like mad. As he went down, the fella was calling Ronnie 'Craig' for some reason and telling him he 'didn't think you was like that. I thought you'd have a straightener, but you need all this lot.'

By that time the few of us who were in the club were running over. Ronnie immediately stopped and spoke calmly to the man.

'I'll have a straightener with you,' he said. 'Come on then, we'll go upstairs.'

The other man scrambled to his feet. He was a big bloke, maybe 6ft 2 or even 6ft 3, fierce eyes. This was George, one of a well-known family called the Dixons, though I'd never met him before. The two of them were halfway up to the gym before Dixon turned around to see that the rest of us were guarding the stairs to ensure that they were left alone. He realised what he was doing to himself

– he was going to lock himself in a room with a complete raving madman of incredible strength and viciousness. With a yell he stopped in his tracks and refused to go further. Ronnie kicked him in the bollocks and he came tumbling all the way down the stairs and he was thrown into the street. That was my introduction to George Dixon and I didn't have that much more to do with him. From what I could tell, he was a bit of a loser really, certainly whenever I saw him he was getting into scrapes.

This kind of encounter was not uncommon in The Double R and for the most part the place kept both twins busy. I didn't see Ronnie do much else, though just once he went on a robbery – and I went with him. I think I must be the only man in the country to say I've been out robbing with Ronnie. Not that he would have done it on his own. He wouldn't be able to find anything to rob to start with. Not a clue, particularly as he didn't drive. But on that one occasion we were in The Regency, a North London club used a lot by all of us, and he got me to get him a motor with a driver.

Albert the Jar's brother, Freddy, was chosen with his big Austin three-way loader van, though we weren't going to travel far for our heist. In the basement under The Regency was a hire purchase place, a tallyman's run by two guys named Gannon and Hamish. According to an old friend of Ronnie's, Dicky Morgan, they had one room filled with stacks of beautiful carpets. At least, that was what this friend said. I hated these tip-offs from Ronnie's old friends. They were the worst people on earth – they had his ear but you couldn't be sure they had the first clue about what they were doing. And you wouldn't be able to get through to Ronnie once he'd got an idea in his head. I had no idea how Dicky Morgan knew they were there, maybe he'd just seen them or something, but he told Ronnie the carpets were worth a fortune.

While Freddy Lovett went to get his motor, the rest of us stayed behind when the club closed up. We broke in downstairs and waited until about seven or eight o'clock in the morning to avoid suspicion before lugging the carpets outside. Ronnie had a contact in Chingford who agreed to have a look at the goods. He only needed one look.

'What have you done?' he asked. 'They're not Indian. They're not Chinese. They're Belgian. A load of rubbish, the whole lot of them. They wouldn't come to 100 quid.'

But though Ronnie called Dicky every name under the sun as we drove away without making a sale, we had actually had a narrow escape. The Chingford fence had just come from doing a long prison sentence and he was soon in all the newspapers. He had what the reporters called 'an Aladdin's cave' of stolen property hidden in a vast secret basement under the house we visited. Despite prison he couldn't stop buying off other criminals – it was an addiction. If we'd been picked up in connection with that load of dodgy old carpets we'd have got about five years each.

It was never going to be through robbery that the twins made their name. They should really have stuck to the clubs. In later years, when The Double R closed, they started on a new venture down the road called The Kentucky. The design of this place was down to their brother Charlie. He was totally different to the twins. He was much more straightforward, a very nice fella. And though that was just my opinion, I never heard anybody say anything about him to the contrary. On the surface he was typical of that kind of East End guy – smart, always had a nice car and he had been a professional boxer. But he wasn't damaged in the sport and I'm sure he would have a better life if he hadn't have been cursed with Ronnie and Reggie for brothers. It was terrible to see him dragged down with them. I have to admit that I saw Charlie at the fights many years later when I got into the business side of boxing and I ducked him. By then I'd been out of contact with the Krays and everyone connected with them for a long time. And Charlie just seemed too sad and I was frightened of embarrassing myself. I just didn't want to see him. I heard from him just once since the Krays went away. He got Ray Moore, his wife's brother who was later shot dead in an unrelated incident, to give me a message – tell Micky I wish I'd gone with him. And I bet he did too. Like his dad, Charlie senior, he didn't deserve to be caught up in the fallout.

It was a couple of years after George Dixon had been kicked in the bollocks at The Double R that I saw him again. I was in a car with Reggie and a couple of others after the club closed one night when we passed him and a fella called Dalison that Reggie had the needle with. They were also in a car. Pulling up in Mile End Road, Reggie stalked back to them.

'Oi, you, come here,' he said. I didn't know the fella Reggie was after or what the problem was. Dixon got out of the car and, rather disloyally, pushed his mate towards Reggie. Maybe it was the lateness of the hour but something about that annoyed me. While Reggie set about punching into Dalison, I striped Dixon.

By then the twins had moved out of Vallance Road and lived in flats above one another in Stamford Hill. I was over at Ronnie's the next day. He wasn't particularly pleased to see me.

'You beat my boyfriend up, didn't you?' he said. I didn't say anything. 'Never mind, Mick', he continued, 'I think that little scar suits him.'

It was odd to hear of Dixon as anyone's 'boyfriend'. Not George Dixon – big, tough guy, leader of the Dixon family. It was a mystery what really went on there. Dixon wasn't known for being gay and – not that it necessarily always means that much – he was married. At a later date Ronnie went on to claim that Dixon had also taken a liberty with him because he knew Ronnie fancied him. This was hardly unusual – Ronnie often had crushes. He was always upset because he never got to meet '60s icon Terence Stamp, for one.

The liberty that George Dixon was accused of taking concerned the Nashes. He'd had a disagreement with them and now he was scared. He'd asked Ronnie to straighten it out for him.

'Yeah, all right,' said Ronnie. 'Just keep out of the way and it'll be all right. I'll sort it out for you. Keep out of the way. Don't be about, don't put me in the middle and I'll sort it.'

He couldn't have been clearer. But then Dixon saw Charlie Kray.

'You know I had a bit of an argument with the Nashes?' he said. 'Has Ronnie done anything about it?'

'I don't know,' said Charlie, fatefully as it turned out. 'Come down to The Regency on Monday morning and I'll ask him.'

The Krays held a regular Monday morning meeting in a room under the club – though there was never much of interest discussed. It was more just to keep a presence. I picked up a pack of cards and started playing pontoon with Nobby Clarke. Aside from all three Kray brothers, present were also Johnny Davies – Ronnie's sometime minder and driver – and notorious associate Freddie Foreman.

Just at that point, Dixon turned up, without saying anything. That was bad enough, though Charlie wasn't to know that Ronnie had specifically told Dixon to keep a low profile. For his part, George hadn't thought to ask Charlie if he'd warned Ronnie that he was coming. He hadn't. The bad part was that George had a mate with him. Nothing was said, though, and Ronnie gave no sign of ill humour as he got up and casually strolled out of the room.

When he returned, Ronnie was running and he had a gun. He put it to Dixon's head and pulled the trigger. Everyone sprang to life, diving towards Ronnie as fast as they could as the gun went click, click, click. Fortunately for Dixon, Johnny Davies – an ex-docker and old friend of mine who had been introduced by me to the twins – took his duties as Ronnie's right-hand man seriously. He had diligently oiled not only the gun but the bullets too. He was always oiling things – 'I am very efficient,' he used to say. The trigger mechanism slipped repeatedly and that was all that saved Dixon's life. Freddie and Reggie wrestled Ronnie, still waving the gun around and incoherent with fury, to the floor.

Charlie shouted, 'Get out!' repeatedly at Dixon, whose mate was standing, stunned and motionless in the unfolding insanity. George himself wasn't in much better condition. He was running like some cartoon character. His feet were going but, dragging his panicked mate behind him, it seemed like he wasn't moving at all. It took them ages to get up the stairs and out. Or maybe it was just time seeming to go slowly while Ronnie raved under the combined weight of his brother and Freddie.

It was a moment to remember and in the years since then plenty of people have claimed to have been there at the time. Others have said it happened somewhere else or didn't happen at all. But the truth was strange enough and I was one of the few who can say I was definitely there to witness it.

Poor old George – still the loser. He even claimed that he made up with Ronnie and that Ronnie gave him the bullet which almost killed him. He said he had it made into a necklace – I didn't see it, but I could believe that.

Another of Ronnie's crushes was actor Billy Murray, who went to find fame as Don Beech in *The Bill*. Unlike Terence Stamp – who the young Murray resembled – Ronnie did get to meet Billy, though he didn't have much more luck with him. Murray was also born in the East End to an Irish father and although he had a couple of fights as a boxer, he was always determined to be an actor. He had the sort of tanned, leading-man looks that appealed to Ronnie.

'Do me a favour, Mick,' he said. 'Will you go and knock on his door and get him out? I don't like to go round there. I don't want his dad to see me.'

I ended up knocking at the door like a kid calling after school.

'Is Billy in, Mr Murray?' But he came out and I told him that Ronnie was sitting out front in a taxi. We went back to Mile End and Ronnie made an excuse to get us over to Dickie Morgan's. His mum allowed Ronnie to bring his boys over and I knew enough to leave them to it. But I was curious to find out how it had gone and asked Ronnie the next day.

'Fucking useless,' said Ronnie. 'He didn't want to know.'

Billy Murray might have been determined to be an actor – but not at *any* price.

George Dixon got into more trouble with his brother Alan when they teamed up with the Berry brothers and started throwing their weight around. I liked Teddy and Checker Berry, former talented boxers, and I was shocked when I heard what happened to Teddy. Details were sketchy to begin with. I was told Teddy had been outside the hospital on Hackney Road when he was shot from behind and one of his legs disintegrated in the blast. He never saw who did it.

The Berrys' father had trained the twins as boxers and both Teddy and Checker had fought professionally in their time. Teddy had been particularly good, though, I was friendly with them both and so were the twins. Checker was charismatic and a good laugh. He drove Ronnie down to Dartmoor on a visit, which he later described to me in memorable terms.

'God, I had a day!' he said when they got back. 'Do you know, Ronnie never spoke one word from Bethnal Green to the nick? We got as far as Exeter, on the edge of the moors somewhere, I was getting really bored and I turned the car radio on. He just leaned forward and turned it off again.'

All we knew about the shooting was what Teddy told us. The attacker came up behind him and brought him down with a shotgun. John Pearson, in one of his books on the Krays, claimed that the twins were behind it and that they bought Teddy a pub as a reward for keeping his mouth shut. But I was with them when they heard the news and they were not only absolutely gobsmacked, but they were annoyed too. They were friendly with the Berrys but there was something of a professional jealousy there – they were the only ones who were allowed to dish out that sort of violence. There was also an element of fear there. What was all of this about?

After the Berrys and the Dixons got together they started to throw their weight around and had a fight outside a late-night drinking club called The Senate Rooms. I'd previously stopped them after they knocked out a guy called Johnny Isaacs. He was laying spark out on the pavement, Checker backed off when I asked him. I wasn't there for the later fight but from what I heard it was over not much more than the usual macho posing.

This time, the fellas that the Berry-Dixon contingent had been fighting at The Senate Rooms had been pretty tasty characters and yet one of them ran away. Not much was thought about that at the time, but it was this same person who came back with a mate and shot Teddy. The twins found out who was behind it and told me, though they didn't do anything about it themselves. The books that claim Teddy was bought off with a pub are wide of the mark, though I wouldn't want to cause poor old Teddy, who is still hobbling about on one leg, any further misery by revealing the name of his attacker here. I can say that it made that person's reputation with the Krays. They were friendly with both parties and that was why it never went any further.

Some people fingered Limehouse Willy. He was an old Kray friend who worked for them in The Spieler and, although he wasn't known for being violent, he did have a fight with Teddy Berry. It was one of those turnouts over nothing but the upshot was that Willy got badly slashed across the face. The rumour was that he was behind the shooting as retribution for the striping, though the truth was he was never like that.

As anyone writing a book should have found out for themselves, the twins settled Willy's grievance in a most ridiculous way. They had a little gambling club called The Greatorex, which was in the heart of Aldgate in Greatorex Street. They organised a bare knuckle fight between a fella called Alfie Barker and Nobby Clarke. The reasoning behind the match was no more than they were both about the same size and Alfie was a friend of Teddy. It was an absurd notion in the first place – having a little fist fight to make up for Willy being cut to ribbons – and it soon descended into farce. Nobby bit Alfie during the match and was disqualified. That was Reggie and Ronnie trying to save face and not make enemies but it was very convoluted. In the end, Limehouse Willy got his own back in a manner of speaking: he would later turn and give evidence against the Krays at their trial.

Chapter Five

Having a Quiet Drink at The Hammer Club

Reggie suggested that he and I both sleep with the stunning girl he was talking to in La Monde, the Chelsea club. She was staying in a flat above the venue. When everyone had gone the three of us trooped into the bedroom. We all got undressed. We got into bed together, gorgeous girl in the middle flanked by me and Reggie. And then we slept together – in the sense that we all went to sleep, got up in the morning and put our clothes back on and we all left.

I wonder what went through her mind. There she was with these two strangers, tough guys and absolutely nothing happened at all. Perhaps she thought that Reggie wasn't interested. But he was very interested and certainly didn't want to go sleep – I doubt any of us got much rest that night. As strange as it sounds for someone with his swagger, Reggie just didn't know what to do next.

He didn't get much further with Vera Day, Forest Gate's answer to Diana Dors. He spotted the starlet in another nightclub when we were out with his old friend Johnny Squibb. Vera was a celebrity back when there weren't the sheer volume you see today and she was quite something, married to East End bodybuilder Arthur Mason. He wasn't with her that night and Reggie invited her over to join us. He soon slid his arm around her, like a teenager who had just gone for his first date in the back row of the cinema.

We all left at 2.00 am and Reggie offered her lift in his beautiful Mercedes. I rode up front with Johnny and Reggie and his new friend sat behind on the way back to her Kensington flat.

'Hang on a second,' said Reggie, 'and I'll just walk Vera to her door.'

It was only a few steps up to the block's entrance hall and Johnny, watching them in the mirror with a grin, began to pull away. As we looked behind us we saw a panicked Reggie desert his charge and come chasing after the car. It was all extremely undignified. Each time he got to the door, Johnny pulled forward again. When Reggie finally got in, panting, he called us every name under the sun. The truth was – as he knew we knew – that despite his bravado, Reggie Kray was terrified of women.

A year before the threesome that never happened, I first noticed the girl that Reggie invited me to sleep with. Me and my friend Jonah discovered her staggering beauty in La Monde, the club ran by Ossie's friend Jamette. The gorgeous girl was clearly out of reach for us, but I remembered her months later when Reggie was chatting to her. I was about to leave when Reggie caught my eye and came rushing over.

'Hang about – you don't want to get away, do you?' He was whispering rather breathlessly. 'We can sleep with that girl tonight, if you want,' he continued. The out-of-reach girl was now a possibility. I hung on until everyone had gone home, but I might as well not have bothered.

Reggie eventually married Frances O'Shea, whose brother I also knew. He had almost the same name, Frank O'Shea. The wedding was a major deal with David Bailey taking the photos. I didn't go – I couldn't stand the carry-on and I was always antisocial. I was snobbish too – there were too many mugs about. Not my scene. It was in Bethnal Green and everyone who'd ever met them even once had come out of the woodwork. I pleaded diplomatic flu. But Reggie didn't mind that I didn't see them until after they got back from honeymoon in Greece. They both joined me for a drink at the El Morocco.

I'd hardly said hello before she said in front of him, 'Do you know he hasn't laid a finger on me in all the time we've been away?'

What do you say in return to something like that? Reggie himself didn't sound angry though, just defeated.

'Cor, I'm glad it's you she's told,' he said sadly, 'and no one else.'

Their marriage was never consummated. Poor old Reggie. His brother's promiscuous antics must have just been just another reminder of his own failures. Ronnie could be very graphic in his physical description of men. He appreciated them like a woman and it used to wind people up. He was always talking about how this person or that old army buddy had 'a lovely body'. Reggie hated all this. He was actually suppressing a gay side of his persona, one that I heard he later reverted to in prison. I guess that in the end he just stopped caring about whether people knew or not.

Esmeralda's Barn provided more prospects for Ronnie to fall for. This club was in the refined environs of Belgravia in a venue that would later be taken over by the Berkeley Hotel. Long before the Krays had even heard of the place it had been very tasteful, with a discerning crowd. The cynical Lord Kilbracken said of fellow punter Lord Effingham's attendance at the House of Lords, 'Do you know, he hasn't missed a sitting since the allowances went up to £4 a day?'

Esmeralda's had a bar where Cy Grant, the resident pianist, would play jazz. It was all very cool. Everyone looked very hip and The Barn's natural market, the Belgravia set, were the height of sophistication. After the Krays took over, you'd sometimes see the Krays' parents, old Charlie and Violet, with their entourage and the generation and class gap was very obvious. Stone-faced, crossed arms, they scowled as if they were on just another East End night out.

Some of the firm would go to The Barn, when they were given permission, but being a bit more freelance I went whenever I liked. Ronnie's personal concerns were still in evidence despite the posh location.

'Oh, Mick, I'm in love,' he sighed one day. 'There's this boy up The Barn. Oh.' He couldn't stop talking about this young man, whose name was Bobby Buckley and when he wasn't talking about him he was taking off his lisping voice. They did get together and I liked Bobby. He wasn't a bad kid.

Away from The Barn but in other West End clubs I could be a bad drunk, sometimes looking for trouble in nightclubs by leaving without paying when the bill came. It wasn't that unusual for people to see me at the end of a night chinning doormen. It wasn't really that malicious, though I might wonder what I'd done when it came to the next morning. I could usually find a grudge that needed to be settled. If there was already something kicking off then so much the better as far as I was concerned.

Then came a couple of fights at The Hammer Club. I was pretty much sober when I fought there and that made me much more of a serious proposition. After that, people started to think I might get out of control. The Hammer was a good place to be seen doing that kind of thing. It was a rough old East End venue which was well named – there were often rows there. You could make yourself a reputation there but it wasn't on turf that was claimed by any of the big firms. The club was in E13 and the twins' influence ended around E3. This was well off their map, all the way down East India Dock Road, along Barking Road and on the turn off onto Greengate Street in Plaistow.

The trouble centred on Johnny Davies. I'd known him since we were both ten when we met at primary school. Even then he was in the morons' class but we stayed friends and I went on to introduce him to the twins. It was him who did such a good job of oiling Ronnie's bullets. Johnny was completely mad at the best of times and now he had become involved in a feud that had come out of nothing more than a fight over a spilled drink at a friend's wedding.

The row started on the Saturday afternoon of the reception and I've still got a photo of some of the guests smiling away with their rosettes prominently displayed. By Sunday lunchtime everyone was fighting again. A fella called Bobby Reading got badly caught up in it. His brother Albert was with the twins in the army doing National Service. Ronnie used to go on about what a marvellous body he had. Back then many people were scared of him and he was a strange character. Albert was once arrested with a gun while dressed as a woman, though he got on well with the local Old Bill. I didn't know him that well and hadn't really grown up under his influence.

The fighting got serious, although nobody was badly hurt until they found one of my pals at home and battered his front door down. But he was ready, lying on the floor with a shotgun, and he blasted them as the door went in. Bobby Reading lost an eye and gained a nickname – 'cockle eye'.

It was carnage. Both sides got arrested and the other side got nine months. Our lot, who didn't have the same influence with the local Old Bill, got three years, including a fella called Bertie Summers who was a good friend of mine.

Albert Reading grassed and they had a friend called Alan Castille who was busy scaring Johnny Davies. Johnny might have been dangerous but he wasn't very brave. You always had to watch the ones like him. Cowards are always more likely to shoot you rather than risk a proper fight. Johnny's family ran a fruit shop and he could generally be found sitting outside it on his apple box, staring into space with one arm resting over his head like a fucking gorilla. He looked like a gorilla too, with a big forehead and a bull neck. He had a proper tough guy appearance, although he wasn't actually a gangster. He was easily spooked and Cassie was making the most of it, coming up and driving him mad. That was what Johnny said when he came crying to me about it, anyway. Equally, he was the type to imagine it all, though he swore to me that he'd been attacked with a chopper. Something had to be done.

The pair of us, Johnny armed with his trusted meat cleaver that made holes in his trousers where he always hid it, and me with my knife, went to find Castille and the rest of them at The Hammer Club. It all sounds very dramatic fare for a Sunday afternoon and it was. Just another lunchtime drink down The Hammer. The enemy were in a big gang with all their mates, including George Dixon. Not all of them were involved, but if they were there that day that was just their bad luck. We polished off our drinks, got up as if to go and then turned at the door and set about them. They scattered in all directions. Some made it to the front door and others hid in the gents. Johnny done Castille on the head with his meat cleaver and he's still got the scar on his face where I striped him.

Roy Shaw, who I'd remembered from the schoolboy boxing championships, was there to hear the little speech I made to the terrified gang, telling them exactly why we were after them and warning them all off by name. Roy was a powerful figure in his own right and he was never shy of causing mayhem when the mood took him. I think he found the whole thing very entertaining.

'I've got my car,' he said afterwards. 'I'll give you a lift.'

It was the start of a friendship between the two of us. Roy had become a legend himself and I soon discovered his character was very much in keeping with the stories of his adventures. An unpredictable man to be around, he was supposed to have been in a borstal where he tied up the psychiatrist and escaped. His appearance matched his reputation with a permanently furrowed brow and endlessly fierce expression. He drank vodka to excess and took purple hearts while keeping himself fit until he eventually succumbed to the lure of steroids. Still a tearaway even today, Roy was recently sectioned.

Roy was in The Hammer again a couple of weeks later when Johnny and I had another fight, this time about a completely unrelated matter. It was over some fellas from Upton Park and it was this fight that made people sit up and take notice of me.

Once again Johnny himself was at the heart of it when his step-brother was attacked in a pub by a bunch of bullies, including such names as Freddy Skennington, the Bennetts – Russy and his brother Pippy – and Georgie Woods. The Bennetts were well known over in Upton Park and they drew a lot of their confidence from their history of being key figures with Jack Spot and Billy Hill. They had a stall on the Queen's Road Market where a lot of the gangsters hung out. Johnny told me all about it and I knew that again we couldn't back down. You couldn't just keep out of the way of families like the Bennetts, otherwise they made your life a misery. I'd heard about them when I was 14 and still at school. Everyone was terrified of them since older brother Porky Bennett did eight years for razor slashing. This threat required an appropriate response. I suggested Johnny get the shooter he had hidden up his chimney – a .45 that he strapped to his leg with big leather clips like an undercover policeman – and I'd get my knife. We'd go back to the club to make a definitive statement.

Russy Bennett was already taunting us. He knew Johnny and I were friends and he warned me about the consequences of the previous fight in The Hammer.

'You're gonna be in trouble,' he said with a smile and his weak laugh. 'You won't like it. I'll guarantee you somebody gets shot around here before too long.' He was right about that.

It was one Sunday a couple of weeks later, just before Christmas that we entered a packed Hammer Club at a time we knew the Bennetts and their mates would be around.

I saw Roy Shaw with one of his friends and as Johnny went off to sit down, I said, 'Do you want to have it away? It's going to be off in here in a minute.'

'No! Course not,' Roy said. 'I've got a gun downstairs in the car. Shall I go and get it for you?'

'No, thanks,' I said. 'We've got one.' That comment ensured I had my new friend for life. For him the imminent row was like standing on the terraces waiting for his favourite football team to come out. Can I play? That's what he was like.

Russy Bennett joined me when I queued at the counter.

'I stuck it on your mate's brother the other night,' he said. This was pure Queen's Road bravado.

'Yeah,' I said. 'Didja?'

'Yeah,' he said. 'How's he feel about it?'

What else could I say? 'Go and ask him.'

Following the script for these sorts of occasions, he sauntered over to Johnny and repeated exactly what he'd said to me. What did Johnny think? I could see what he thought as he went for the gun. I knew he would, this was classic Johnny. As strange as it may sound, it was quite funny. I was excited and I was looking forward to it kicking off. The Queen's Road mob were major names and we were going to strike at them hard.

Davies didn't use his gun, not at first. 'You bastard!' he yelled and threw a punch at Russy. Two of Russy's mates dived in and it was soon a bit of a melee, much more so than our previous fight. I joined in with my knife, taking a swing at anyone and everyone who came near enough. I cut Freddy, slashed him across the cheek so hard it almost took his head off.

Then Pippy Bennett punched me in the head and made me drop the blade. I looked around. A group of mates drinking in there had just had a collection for a crate of beers to share around. I reached down, and grabbed them – later I would get a few moans from those who contributed to the crate, especially Fatty Gray– I smashed all of them one by one over Pippy's head and cut him. Some people later called it a scalping. By this time Johnny had his .45 out. He shot Russy in the bollocks and, though we didn't know it at the time, only narrowly missed the crucial femoral artery. He also established a lasting reputation for himself for being what I already knew he was – a madman. All the pre-Christmas drinkers made a scramble for the exits at the same time. You've never seen a place empty so quickly.

We'd won the victory we needed. I had to get out and be sure not to look as if I was in any kind of hurry. I didn't want to draw any attention to myself once I was out of the club. I vaguely recognised someone else going down the stairs at the same time as me and tried to engage him in conversation.

'What happened up there?' I asked innocently. He had obviously seen what I'd been up to and could only stare at me in shock and horror. So much for the casual exit.

I legged it to Esmeralda's Barn to find the twins, taking my time to ensure that I wasn't followed. Only Ronnie was there. I told him what had happened and I knew he would understand. For the Krays, all kinds of shootings and similar rows were most welcome. As long as we won. They provided good war stories over a drink and they were just good PR.

'I've got to find somewhere safe now,' I said.

'Well, you're in luck,' he said. 'We've taken a flat off someone over a debt.'

It was the fag-end of a lease, not that Ronnie knew anything about how property worked. It just happened to work in our favour. The owner was a funny little fella called David Litvinoff. He was a journalist who worked on the William Hicky column in *The Daily Express*. I had seen him around, though I didn't know him personally. His hair was very thin, he dressed quite well and if it might be stretching the point to say that he was Bobby Buckley's previous boyfriend, as a much older man he did apparently play the role of sugar daddy. It wasn't a secret – he was completely out of the closet at a time when it was still very much illegal and while he wasn't effeminate, he didn't give a fuck who knew he was gay.

As we talked over the details of the hideaway we were joined by Davies. The two of us had been split up in the race to get away from the scene of the fight. Somehow he met up with our mutual friend who got him safely to The Barn.

Davies had been impressed by my performance. He said, 'Never get in a fight when you're drunk. You're useless. But up The Hammer Club you were sensational – when you were sober.'

He made a lot of sense; it just wasn't something that I had considered before. Since then I've tried to stick to his words as much as I could.

Litvinoff's flat was in South Kensington at number 7 Ashburn Place, just off Cromwell Road. It was the last place anyone would think to look for us.

'I'll see you there,' Ronnie said.

It was the break we needed. He insisted we could stay as long as we needed, which ended up being something like six months.

There was a bit of a hue and cry on after the row with headlines in *The Daily Mail* but I missed it all while I was out of sight. When the story was later written up in the media I didn't recognise any of it. It didn't happen the way others have said. From what I later heard, the press once more made out that the Hammer fight was all about protection rackets. It made good copy and was more interesting than the truth – that most rows were over precisely nothing at all. Or at least, nothing important. The sad reality was that you were more likely to see a fight because someone simply wanted to throw their weight around. But that didn't sell as many newspapers and books as claiming that gangs were taking over London and no small business was safe. If only anyone was that organised we'd have all made a lot more money.

The most valuable thing to come out of the two fights for me was reputation – I was now known as someone who was not to be underestimated. I was convinced that we had got away with it as far as the law was concerned as well, but I was wrong. Some ten years later I would be nicked and done two-handed with Johnny for attempted murder.

The turnout at The Hammer was important for another reason. It marked the end of one era of gangster and the rise of another. The likes of Jack Spot were history and they were beginning to decline and now their supporters among the Queen's Road mob looked vulnerable too. The Krays were the next wave and I was coming up with them. The Hammer was the tipping point. It was a direct challenge to the old guard.

I was to see the effects for myself not long after I came out of hiding. I clearly remember the first morning leaving my house. I lived in Rochester Avenue, just off Queen's Road, more or less within sight of the market. I had to pass the mob's stalls on the way to the station. Just my presence was a challenge. Having won the battle at The Hammer Club I was full of confidence and, just as they had relied on Jack Spot and Billy Hill, I had the Krays' name to give me strength. But I wasn't stupid, whenever I did the walk I always carried a little shooter in my pocket.

The moment I was always half expecting came one Sunday afternoon when I stopped by The Queen's for a drink. After the pub closed for the afternoon I had a chat with Stevie Tucker outside my house nearby. None other than Pippy Bennett happened to be passing with another fella, Harold Reagan. Me and Stevie were sat in a van on the side of the road and when Pippy got to the end of the street he and Reagan turned around and started back towards us. I was ready. I'd had enough time to slip back indoors and pick up a machete. I waited until they got near before jumping out of the van and steaming towards them with the weapon. They fled, screaming. And that was the moment I knew everything had changed.

If I'd done that to a member of the Bennett family in the middle of Queen's Road before The Hammer Club I'd have been strung up from a lamp post. Anyone in the area would know what this latest encounter meant – word would soon get around and the mob would lose respect. Stevie Tucker, who I had been with that afternoon, went on to see Dicky, another member of the Bennett family. When Dicky heard what happened he immediately realised the importance and he was furious – but frustrated. There wasn't anything he could do and soon it wasn't just the writing that was on the wall.

'He picked his dinner up,' Stevie said, 'and threw it across the room.'

Dicky's food dripped down onto his carpet, marking the end of an era. The Upton Park mob fell apart after that. A few faces were quick to tell me they were on my side, though I had no intention of starting a war with anyone. Basically, they were all soon having a go at each other. But gangsters were like that – that's why they were gangsters. As soon as things got difficult they were at each other.

Johnny Davies got very cocky when it became clear that the balance of power had shifted decisively in our favour. He walked into The Bongo Club in Canning Town with Jacky Bowers, whose brother Wally, even though he had an arm in plaster, had recently been attacked by Georgie Woods and his crew. John stabbed Georgie Woods in the throat for his part in the attack on both their brothers. He had a velvet collar on his overcoat and he would go to Queen's Road Market and out-dazzle all the gangsters on the square. Freddy Foreman's brother, George, had a club in Clapham. Davies was dancing there with his girlfriend one night when Joey Carter, an ex-boxer, touched him up the arse. Carter had a fighter's flat nose and was quite a sight as Johnny turned to see who was making fun of him.

'Did you like that?' asked Joey. 'I thought you'd like it.'

'Bollocks,' replied Johnny Davies. Joey punched him in the mouth and Johnny pulled out a knife and cut him to ribbons.

This was a major problem for Freddy Foreman. He was very friendly with Joey and apart from anything else, Johnny's savage attack had happened in Foreman's brother's club. A full Kray meeting was held the next day.

It was very awkward. This was a real Judgement of Solomon moment. Nobody knew what to do for the best. The twins came up with one of their classic fudges – Johnny Davies was to be formally sacked from their firm. It meant nothing but all anyone wanted was a way out without losing face and all sides went along with it. Everyone except Johnny himself. He came to see me and was complaining bitterly about what had happened and wanted me to help him even the score, as he saw it. I paid very little attention to what he was saying. He was just being annoying and I told him to get on with it himself.

He left my house with a friend of ours, Davey Storey, who came back alone, minutes later, looking very shook up.

'Johnny's just shot himself,' he said. What? I thought. I hadn't meant for him to think I was being harsh. I just hadn't been in the mood for his aggressive nonsense. But before I could feel too guilty, Davey explained that Johnny had a gun in his pocket which he was just playing around with as they were out on the street and it had accidentally gone off. 'He's shot himself in the leg,' said Davey.

'Oh, bring him in!' I said.

We eventually dispatched a hobbling Johnny to see Dr John, the local drunkard we all used for occasions like this.

'Och,' said the doctor when he saw him. 'You're a brave wee laddie.'

I was soon back to life as normal with the Krays. Back when Johnny and me had been in hiding in Litvinoff's flat, David Litvinoff himself came to see us. He'd struck me as quite naive, a bit out of his depth compared to the characters we usually hung around with. For someone who had been around as long as he had he was unwise in calling Ronnie 'bottlenose' as often as he did. Once was too much, for a start. But the pair of them were competing for the affections of Bobby Buckley and love had obviously made Litvinoff stupid as well as blind. He was far too open in his opinion about Ronnie's choice of young men.

'I can't work out what role Ronnie plays in this,' he confided. He was very well spoken and chose his words carefully. 'He certainly doesn't father them,' he said. The puzzle occupied him for a while, but by the next visit he'd worked it out.

'He takes the woman's role!' he said triumphantly. 'He likes to *mother* them!'

When Ronnie was later in the nick he would go on to try to adopt children. It was an instinct inside him. I've often thought about where all of that came from – it was irresistible, coming up with theories for the twins' extreme characters. Knowing their famously devoted mother you might want to play amateur psychologist and put Ronnie's extraordinary antics down to her influence. She was a funny old thing and she was exactly like Ron – cooing and clucking over her sons. But to be honest, I don't know. I really don't know. I was friends with them for years and I would still hesitate to claim to understand what made them tick, much less work out the roots of their sexuality. It's only something I've thought about afterwards. At the time, motives weren't so important to me. Litvinoff himself might also have done well to consider the danger he was putting himself in with his speculating. Ronnie eventually got someone to walk up to his love rival and slash him across the face in the street.

Whatever the reason for Ronnie's behaviour, at last it made sense to me now that Litvinoff had shared his insight. I began to think that maybe something more had gone on with George Dixon. If Ronnie preferred the female role, perhaps he'd given Dixon a blow job. It would make sense – Dixon was such a giant, so masculine, that it couldn't have been anything else. There was undeniably a pattern to how Ronnie behaved and now I knew what to look for. I'd seen it often enough.

Say he was in The Grave Maurice pub and in came some boy he was trying to seduce. He would beckon them over.

'Come on, come on,' he would say. 'Come and sit down. What are you having?' He was very charming when he wanted to be. But he would invariably turn to me and, adopting a simpering tone, say something like, 'Look at his eyes, Mick! Ain't he lovely?'

'Oh, shut up, Ron,' the boy would say.

'Oh – but you are! Look at you! Aren't you lovely!' He scared off boxer Terry Spinks like that. Ronnie kept trying to pull him and when he wasn't harassing him personally he kept a photo of him which he would coo over. He was like a fond grandmother even in front of his mates in public, scratching at the image with his finger and proudly pointing out Spinks's cutest features to his largely horrified audience. He made me laugh, though he would go on and on until it got on our nerves.

Steff had the answer for him. 'I just haven't got the glands to appreciate it, Ron.'

He never knew when to stop and if he did indeed have a mothering instinct, it came together with a love of very sinister theatrics. At the end of Hitchcock's *Psycho*, an insect lands on Anthony Perkins' hand and as he glances down at it he says, 'I wouldn't hurt a fly.' Ronnie appreciated the undertones of that line. It was his favourite in any film. He was always quoting it.

You could see his personality in the clubs the twins ran, particularly Esmeralda's. It was undeniably louche, very sleazy, very dangerous. The punters who came to gamble did so partly to lurk in the shadows cast by the lighting arrangements, which were designed to look as intimidating as possible. Ronnie, even more than his brother, knew the value of special effects. The cloak of menace that hung over the tables at The Barn impressed a crowd which included the likes of painter Lucian Freud as well as Lords Kilbracken and Effingham.

The aristocracy were famously attracted to the Krays. Lord Boothby was one of their most prominent fans. It had been widely rumoured that he had an affair with Ronnie, but there was no substance to the story. Boothby had come into contact with the twins through a lad from Hoxton named Lesley Holt. He had come to meet a mate at the billiard hall many years earlier. This was long before the Krays had any kind of notoriety. It was Albert the Jar who pointed him out to me.

'You see that kid over there?' he whispered to me. 'He's been having an affair with Lord Boothby. He was telling us what he does. Boothby makes them pull their trousers down, bends them over and smacks their arses with a slipper!'

The lord was hardly someone to be mothered by Ronnie, but it was true that they were introduced – through Lesley. There wasn't anything more than that to the Boothby legend and the papers had nothing more to go on than a photo of Boothby with Ronnie. This they had probably got from the twins themselves, who wouldn't have been above having a bit of an earner out of themselves passing it over. Fame was always a motivating force for them. More than power, and much more than money.

Nobody else was allowed to enjoy publicity. It was okay for the twins to be interviewed and featured, but they would get very jealous when someone else even took the smallest step into the limelight, as local car dealer Connie Nunn found out. He was the centrepiece of some tabloid article about snatching back cars. I'm not even sure if he wrote it himself or was just featured, but the sight of his face staring out of a big article enraged the twins.

'It's grassing, innit,' they said to each other. 'He's a fucking grass, ain't he? He's going to be dead.' And yet Reggie would still be giving interviews and writing books as he lay on his deathbed.

Celebrity seemed to find the twins even when they weren't looking for it. Once Reggie travelled with Johnny Squibb to Sweden to watch Floyd Pattison fight. Like me, the twins never lost their interest in boxing. There were a couple of very smart Americans who caught Reggie's eye at the ringside. They really looked the part and made quite an impression on him, though he didn't talk with them at that point. But he remembered them when he saw one of the same men some time later in a London club called The Astor. Ever the gent, Reggie approached him and confirmed it was indeed the same man.

'Did you have a nice time?' Reggie asked. His new friend had and the two were soon having a drink together.

The fella was an American lawyer with many high-profile clients. He was extremely well connected. Reggie had lucked out, though he had no idea at all of how good a contact book his companion had and was only being friendly when he said, 'Look us up if you're ever back in London. Or if you ever have any friends you want looked after, we'd be pleased to meet them.'

This was the famous Kray charm and Reggie meant it. This was nothing to do with crime or money – they didn't only invite people to visit their clubs simply to belt them, though that wasn't unusual either.

The lawyer took Reggie at his word and correctly guessed that his clients would be well cared for and would find the twins absolutely fascinating. He directed a stream of American celebrities towards the Krays, up to and including Judy Garland. I saw her myself at The Palladium with her daughter Liza Minnelli. Later, Judy joined us with her then husband Mark Herron at one of the Krays' locals in the East End. It was an unlikely location for the superstar, though she didn't seem to be in a fit state to care much. She was on serious drugs, frail and thin. She looked terrible. There was nothing of her.

The pub was one of those pokey old buildings with the bar counters separated by a wood partition topped with a sliver of window. It was an old man's boozer, where respectable elderly couples would come for a quiet drink. But that night everyone knew the special guest. Curious heads peered over the partition, yet nobody came in the bar itself. Not that it was locked, but somehow people wanted to be in her presence without actually stepping in. It was all very surreal, especially when the rest of the bar spontaneously broke into a hearty rendition of an old classic, the lyrics altered into the plural so as not to make anyone feel left out – 'For They Are Jolly Good Fellows'.

And the stars kept coming. Frank Sinatra Jr arrived with a minder who would look standard issue these days but back then really stood out. Eddie Pucci, a hulking ex-American football player of inevitable Sicilian descent, who was later found dead, riddled with bullets on a golf course in America. Pucci lost no time in reminding Ronnie of his charge's heritage. The twins were starstruck and were straight in there, bulbs flashing, endless matey photos. Visiting the Krays became the thing to do for a certain portion of the American elite. Barney Ross, an old-world champion boxer, was among those who visited Vallance Road and got a tour of the tiny streets packed into that area of the East End. I was charged with getting him there.

'Bring him all the way through Spitalfields Market,' said Ronnie, 'in the dark.'

It was that theatrical side coming out again. He knew that the deserted rows of stalls at night would be a delightfully spooky way to greet the visitor. Ross got a flavour of the East End that many were fascinated by and most people never got to see.

Another American boxing legend who visited was Sonny Liston. He didn't come via Reggie's lawyer friend, however, but was hired by the twins to be at one of their functions at The Cambridge Rooms, a venue out by Kingston to the south of London. Liston didn't really know what he'd got himself into. He had a manager who agreed to let him be the guest of honour for a fee, the money being more important than who would be at the club. I'm sure Liston regretted letting his management make this particular booking for him. The night itself was not much documented. For some reason the press had taken against giving the Krays publicity and even though many of their celebrity fans turned out, there was hardly a mention in the newspapers.

Women clustered around Liston, who proved to be quite a hit. They included Dolly, Charlie Kray's wife. Ronnie already hated her, just as he did Frances. He convinced Charlie that flirting with Sonny Liston was somehow showing up the Kray family name. I've got a photo of the twins with me and I'm looking out of the shot – over to the phone booth outside the room where Dolly had crashed over, fighting with Charlie. It was a typical evening out for the Krays, but not for poor old Sonny Liston. He knew enough about gangsters from brushes with the Mafia in America and realised exactly what he'd got himself into. He was terrified.

Reggie drove us home afterwards, with Sonny and a couple of his friends in the back. The boxer was used to facing racial harassment from the police back home and he could see that Reggie was drunk. He was even more nervous.

'Has Reggie been to the States?' he asked.

'He hopes to go soon, Sonny, but he hasn't been yet,' I said.

'So why he is driving on the fucking right-hand side?' snapped Liston. 'I'm gonna do what the guy did when he fell off the truck, *Hit the Road Jack.*'

He spent the whole journey looking around for police cars, convinced we would be pulled over.

Chapter Six

In Danger in The Kentucky

It felt as if the ground shifted under my feet. I was in The Kentucky Club with Ronnie and had mentioned the name of a friend we both knew but for some reason he took my innocent remark to be a trick. Even then I didn't quite realise how much danger I was in.

'That's not the name you told me last time, is it Mick?' Ronnie said.

This could be trouble. One minute we were passing time, just talking about a charge I'd been fitted up with. It didn't even concern Ronnie. Now he doubted my every word, even the name of the person I was nicked with.

'Yeah,' I said. 'Lenny Stringer.'

'No, that ain't the name,' he said. 'You told me a different name. What's it all about?'

'What? I didn't!' I said. 'That ain't about anything.'

'You're doing this for a reason, aren't you?' he said, but without raising his voice. 'You think I'm a grass, don't you? Everybody's going around saying that Reggie and me are grasses.' I felt the trellis work by the wall behind me in The Kentucky Club's bar. Any second now he was going to punch me straight through it.

The evening had taken a sudden turn from the pleasant social encounter it had started as. When we met there weren't even many customers in the club, it was really just me and Ronnie. He bought me a gin and tonic and I was just gossiping more than anything else.

'Got three months today, Ron,' I said. And then the words that for some reason got him so angry: 'Do you remember I told you about when we got nicked over the offensive weapons with old Lenny Stringer?'

I made it worse after he said that everyone thought he was a grass. Even then I hadn't realised how deep the waters were with him that day. I wasn't paying attention to the way he was talking, just to the facts of what he said.

I dismissed his concern: 'Don't worry, they say that about all club owners, you don't want to take no notice of all that, do you?'

Now Ronnie was off, raving incoherently. That was when I really thought he was going to smash me. But his rant was interrupted by the arrival of someone else we knew and, once he was distracted, I was able to seize the opportunity to go around the trellis and out the door.

I couldn't be sure that he'd forgotten about it when I went over to Vallance Road the next night. A bigger group of us were going to go to The Kentucky again but Ronnie asked me to hold back.

'Hang on a minute, Mick, I'll have a walk down there with you,' he said.

That wasn't out of character for him, although it might sound sinister given what had only just happened. Ronnie wanted me on my own. Of course, I was wary, but then I always was when Ronnie was around. I wasn't cocky, but the rule had to be the same as around a wild animal. I could never get myself comfortable around him, but I also couldn't show any concern. In that respect this was like any other evening. We walked down Vallance Road together in the night air, just the two of us, towards Whitechapel.

'Mick,' said Ronnie softly, 'I'm sorry about the other night. You must think I'm a right prat.' I'd never heard him say those words before – two sentences relating to himself with 'sorry' and 'prat' in them.

'No,' I said, 'that's all right, Ron.'

'Nah, I'll tell you what's happened. I've been experimenting with my medication. I've left it off for a few days. I'm taking it again now. But when I wasn't…I can't describe it to you. Everything was like a fog. It's really strange.'

In my own dealings with people who've had mental health problems in later years, I've come across that description more than once. The idea that you're in fog is common. Many find it hard to get the feeling across.

'Look,' he said, holding out a hand filled with tablets, 'there's the pills I take. Do you want one? You can take one.'

It was like a kid sharing candy. 'Yeah,' I said, 'Give us one!' I had no wish to taste what was called Stelazine, an anti-psychotic, but it was just to show a bit of goodwill. I gulped down his freebie and that was the end of the matter. One dose of the drug had no effect on me but at that time not much did. I was soon washing it down with a nice gin and tonic at The Kentucky and we went on with our evening as the best of friends. Ronnie was stable and the incident was never mentioned again.

The prison sentence we had been discussing the previous night had been hanging over my head for a while. I had been arrested some time before while giving a lift to my friend, old Lenny Stringer. I was in a car with a friend when I saw the conman who had done six years down The Moor – one of the few unfortunate enough to get caught at the corner – and I had to stop for a few words when I saw him down Queen's Road. He was like an uncle to me. As I drove him home, we were boxed in by two big Humber cars. Forced to pull up, we were told to get out by men in suits who turned out to be Scotland Yard's Flying Squad. We were scurfed – grabbed – and bundled into one of the waiting police cars.

I didn't like the look of what was on the floor in the back of the car. A crowbar wrapped in brown paper. Lenny the old boy was in a different car as the three of us were taken to West Ham Police Station. Not a word was spoken as we were taken down to the cells, even when I got my fingerprints taken. But I knew what had led to us being picked up. If you were pulled in and you didn't know what it was you were supposed to have done, it was usually because some other criminal had put the finger on you. I just didn't know the details and so I asked a real mug's question. 'What's it all about?' That was such a clichéd question to ask. So many mugs come out with it when they've been chinned that it's something of a saying. But I came out with it and a Welsh-sounding officer had an answer for me.

'The manor will be a bit fucking quieter without you, boyo.'

Somebody wanted me and my friend off the streets. This had to have gone back to The Hammer Club fight. The row might have made my name but it also made me enemies. I was a nuisance now, too big for my boots. Somebody wanted to take me down a few notches and to this day I don't know who it was who set me up. All I was able to find out later was that the source of the trouble lay with the relations of those who had been hurt in The Hammer.

We were all slung back in our cells until the police were ready to let us have it.

'You are charged with possession of the following offensive weapons: an iron bar, stockings, two bits of celluloid and a cosh.'

The bar was the crowbar and the celluloid was used for opening Yale locks. The cosh was a length of rubber hose. We were in the hands of Scotland Yard's Flying Squad. Frank Williams was the Welshman and the squad's second-in-command. He was also a very good friend of Freddie Foreman, which would later be the cause of a fight between him and Frankie Fraser when he accused Foreman of being a grass.

With the offensive weapons laid out in front of us, the three of us heard the charges. Then we were taken back our cells and I began to feel a bit sick. I was convinced this wouldn't be the end of it. We would end up on a charge of conspiracy to robbery and I thought, I'm going to get five years here. Each in our separate the cells we talked amongst ourselves in a mixture of Gypsy and Yiddish and slang that would have been virtually incomprehensible to anyone listening in.

The gist of it was that the other fella that Stringer and me were with, said, 'Don't worry about it. I can get this watered down and we can straighten it. We'll give them a few quid.'

For the first time I felt a bit of hope. He seemed confident.

'Today?' I asked.

'Yeah, we'll get bail soon.' That could be handy.

My friend offered £200 to the Flying Squad to keep the charge at possession of offensive weapons. The police would also not verbal us, meaning that they wouldn't say that we'd admitted we were going out to burgle somewhere or carry out some major robbery. Bail was duly granted and at the Magistrates' Court two of us pleaded guilty – another part of the agreement – while Lenny Stringer was acquitted because we'd only been giving him a lift.

I felt I had just about successfully negotiated an occupational hazard. If you had friends and a bit of luck you could usually make your way around these sorts of things. You just had to keep your eyes open. That same night at The Kentucky I forgot to follow my own advice and that was when Ronnie cornered me. Having survived the encounter with him and accepted his unexpected apology, I went back to court to drop my appeal.

My friend and I appeared at West Ham's quarter sessions and were sent to Pentonville Prison to serve the time. The jail term wasn't, really, a big deal. I never found out who was behind the fit up and I wouldn't have gone after them even if I had. I'd have settled for hating them from a distance. Should whoever was behind the fit up come within range, well, it might be different. But I certainly wouldn't have gone after them. The police were the guv'nors at that time and I couldn't ignore the fact that someone had serious influence with them. If they were prepared to fit me up for robbery, what would they do if I escalated the feud? I would just be arrested for something else.

The twins suffered from the same problem a lot. There was one crooked woman who swore blind that she caught Reggie breaking into her home. She was probably completely mad, but there was a load of aggravation for Reggie in getting out of that. It was all too easy to get into the criminal justice system if someone made a complaint. But getting out was very difficult. You had to see it through the whole process.

It's hard to overstate how much power the police had back then. It's so different now, when you can often see young people – women as well as men – talking back to officers on the street. They know that now the police can't just do anything they want. Back then there were no limits. You could go away for a long time just for being in the way. If you were crooked, that was enough. You didn't need to have done the crime. Sometimes the police were just downright incompetent, but there was nothing you could do about it. We just got on with our lives and treated them like a force of nature. You could see the storm coming, but there wasn't a lot you could do if it hit you.

Two men I personally knew were sent away for a long stretch when they were completely innocent. I first read about it in an *Evening Standard* report of an armoured car robbery in Longfleet, Kent. Some £87,000 had been stolen; an impressive amount and one of my friends knew the mob who were behind it. We all got to hear about it in time. There wasn't much to it. I knew Roy Shaw was involved. He was on the dole at the time but was soon cruising around in a white Mercedes sports car – so at least he got something out of it.

The robbery was just a fact on the manor and everyone knew who was really behind it. But the police didn't seem to have a clue. They whirled around, pulling in all sorts of people and questioning them down at Plaistow station. Yet of the five suspects eventually charged, only two were involved. Roy and one other. Another fella got acquitted, but the two men I got to know – who I will call Bill C and Bill S – were innocent.

I became friendly with Bill C years later and he told me that his problem had been that he knew the robbers. The firm warned him to steer clear of them as they were being watched. But he was young and didn't think he had anything to worry about. He didn't know how careful you had to be when the police were looking to get someone.

Bill S was more of a mystery to most people. He was from the Elephant & Castle – or over the water, as we called any place south of the Thames – and I only knew him through the friends I'd made there with my friend Ronnie Curtis. Most people on the manor who didn't travel around as much as I did had no idea who he was. Bill S was an upright-looking fella of above average height, about 5ft 10–5ft 11 and he could have passed for a policeman himself. As he sat in their cell, the others stayed at the other end. They wouldn't talk to him.

In court the jury heard how the armoured truck used a road which passed a piece of green where the robbers staged a bit of a kick about with a football. It meant they avoided standing on the street corner looking like gangsters. A policeman passing on a bike happened to see the game and gave a description of a 5ft 8 man with a big mop of hair. As the judge summed up the case he told the jury that Bill C wouldn't have looked his full height if he'd been dashing around the football green. And perhaps his straight hair would have been flying around. It was hardly conclusive. Bill S had been buying long-firm gear – goods obtained through fraud – in his area.

When the police raided Bill S's house they found a significant sum of money in the shoebox in his wardrobe and some more in his wife's handbag. Bank clerks used to sign off on a sticker on the bundles of notes and a signature found on a note at Bill S's place was said to match the missing money. That was all the evidence there was. It didn't matter. A couple of soppy pieces of circumstantial evidence were enough to do for those two.

The lesson from that was the only way to deal with the police was to keep out of their way entirely. If they wanted you badly enough, they'd get you. Each of the four in the Longfleet case got 15 years.

Bill C recalled, 'I sat in the cell under the court after I got the 15 and my legs wouldn't stop shaking.' I had to feel some sympathy – these were incredibly long terms. It was a foretaste of what the Great Train Robbers could expect later in the 1960s. They were given 30-year stretches.

I would later get to know Bill C when a friend of mine asked me to visit him in Dartmoor Prison. As my friend was on the run, I took his place and Bill told me more about his story. I was determined to do what I could to help him get out. Through a solicitor I got to meet columnist Jeremy Hornsby on *The Daily Express*. He took up the campaign. Between us we would eventually got Bill C parole but not until he'd done eight years.

It wasn't uncommon to try and help people out when they got sent down. If nothing else, there was often a collection for the aways, which was mainly done to further the twins' PR. When I did my time after being fitted up, the Krays organised one for me – though I never saw any of the money. They gave it to Tommy Hume, a small, thin man who lived down Custom House in a prefab. He was always conning people and he used to run about like a rat. There was always someone after him. A sickly man, he came down with tuberculosis but he didn't care a fuck for anybody and when Ronnie asked me if I had got the money from him, I knew immediately that he would have spent it himself. Hume ended up in a chest hospital and nobody had the heart to sort him out. It was even suggested that we go and see him when it sounded as if he might not survive. But then another one of the Krays' associates vetoed the idea.

'Think about it,' he warned. 'He may get better.' Oh, yeah, everyone thought. And he never got another mention. And he didn't get better either.

I haven't talked much about my family life and I want to keep that personal side of things out of this book as much as possible. I will say that it was around this time, 1961, that my son Michael was born. His mother, my wife, was one of the Queen's Road mob from Upton Park and I got to know her through being friendly with them. Having grown up in the area, she knew everyone, including those who would go on to be the bosses. But our relationship was a huge mistake. We didn't get on from day one and we had a very quiet marriage in a register office, staying together for the child, at least at first. We were together for ten years.

I didn't want Michael growing up with what was then still the stigma of having unmarried parents. But my wife and I lived our lives completely independently from the day we got married. She barely knew the Krays and of the twins themselves, only Ronnie came to visit our place and that was only once.

For most of our marriage we lived in the area in which she'd grown up. There was a brief period we spent abroad – I had to go to Spain in a hurry. It was out there that she first became ill and had to go onto dialysis. I decided to stay with her and we remained together throughout the long treatment. But by the time she died following a kidney transplant, we had finally agreed to separate. That is all I really want to say about that side of my life – I did meet someone else in 1979 and we're still together now, though we were never married.

At first I brought home money from the corner and the jars, but it was never as much or as easy as the living I began to make when I ran long-firm frauds. We called them LFs for short. This work kept me off the streets and it meant that I could at last start to get in some serious cash. It was still a con, though. The idea was that you rented some premises, registered a company and built up good references under its name. You processed as many goods as possible by selling them under cost, but you always paid the bills promptly. You then exploited the good name of the firm to get goods in on credit before selling them off quick without paying for them, shutting the doors and disappearing.

I didn't actually do the frauds, but I managed the fella who did, Bill Stansill. It was rather a strange appointment by the twins, getting two conmen to look after their money. Not a safe business move to leave us in charge. Though it has to be said there wouldn't have been any takings at all were it not for me babysitting the twins so they didn't take all the money out of the firms before the fraud could be built up. I was with Ronnie when he visited an LF which had nothing to do with me.

Ronnie said, 'How's it going?' The two fellas who worked the firm ran through what they'd paid, what they hadn't paid and what they might be able to order if they paid someone else a certain amount.

'Yeah,' sighed Ronnie. 'Show me.' They got the money out, Ronnie scooped it all up, stuffed it in his pockets and looked directly at me. 'A bird in the hand is worth *five* in the bush, Mick. Come on, let's go.'

Of course, that meant the scheme collapsed before any money had been properly earned. I used to have to distract Ronnie from getting involved at all or manage the far more difficult trick of convincing him that he could make thousands more if he just let it build up. But neither brother had much patience to let things develop. It wasn't easy, but it was safer and more lucrative work than my other cons.

The twins knew I was smarter than most and that was why they needed me but they didn't know – or preferred to ignore the fact – I slipped off out of their sight to run my own LFs. They had me around to make sure nobody was ripping them off and yet I was the very one who was doing it. Right under their noses. I was lucky they were short-sighted. They would send me to check on any rumours of rival action.

I was even dispatched to the north of England, to Bishop Auckland, to check out a story that someone was working a rival LF. That the twins were prepared to go so far away from their home territory showed how seriously they took the business. I made sure I was particularly careful to hide my own actions, both from the Krays themselves and anyone who might get the word back to them. They might not have been that clued up but had they even had a sniff of what I was up to I wouldn't have been seen again. I was under no illusions and I knew this was just one more reason why I could never relax around them.

I also had to make sure that I didn't leave any evidence for the police. I was scrupulous about covering my tracks and this would serve me well when I was later charged in the general conspiracy with the Krays. I never signed for goods or received money. I had no contact with the Krays' financial adviser, Leslie Payne – who later gave evidence against them – and he never paid me for anything. I knew I was ahead of everyone else – I was just extremely confident. That's one of the reasons writing this book is such a departure for me. At last I'm recording it all. I'll probably get 100 years or something.

Chapter Seven

A SEARCH FOR THE BODY AT THE GLENRAE HOTEL

The Krays trusted me with their long-firm frauds and I took advantage of that. I was never too greedy and I was always careful. They never suspected I was ripping them off and when they wanted someone to go to France, they turned to me.

A Lebanese gold buyer in Paris had acquired the proceeds from a bullion robbery. The twins asked me to go over to France to see if I could 'corner' him somehow, although in reality it was a just a trip for fun. Bill Stansill came with me, though he wasn't quite the conman he thought he was. He had the personality for it but at the same time he was that much older and you needed to be a bit more agile to do well in that game. It didn't matter too much for the lightweight job and I certainly didn't take our trip very seriously. We just took the expenses out of the LF we were working on and stayed at The George V Hotel in Paris. And we made sure we lived well. I'd never been to the city before and I had the time of my life.

We'd got some muscle with us in the shape of a fella called Buller Ward. He came from the Angel in London and I didn't like him at all. Just a fucking gorilla. His nickname told you everything you needed to know – he was really called Sidney. Buller came from a family of four brothers and the others were all right. One of them moved to France during the war, married a local girl and was to all intents and purposes a Frenchman, with children who were completely French. We stayed with Buller's brother for one night while we were out there.

The trip was all very enjoyable, though Buller's presence was entirely unnecessary. We didn't need protection. If anything, Paris might have done with some help to deal with us – we were out for the best of everything and as many French birds as we could get. And we were doing it with someone else's money. I'd always wanted to go to Paris, I've been back dozens of times since, but I don't think anything could top that first trip.

After the trip I was making one of my regular visits to Vallance Road with Bill when I saw a red car with a cream roof, a Hillman Hunter estate. Something about it held my attention. I don't know what it was. Maybe it slowed when it didn't need to or turned around. Later on that same day when we were out at an LF in Chingford, I thought I saw it again. It had to be the same car. Yes, I realised, when I saw it do the same manoeuvre – driving slowly, turning around and coming back for no apparent reason. Now I couldn't keep it to myself.

'I saw that motor this morning round the twins',' I told Bill. I knew what it meant. 'That's Old Bill.' Bill, however, had seen nothing.

'Nah, what are you talking about?' he said. 'Shuddup.' I've had that a few times when I've spotted things. But I was observant and one of the things I noticed was that people like to be in denial when there's something uncomfortable in front of their faces. I would naturally spot those sorts of things when even supposedly smart guys would prefer to blank it out – and to ridicule me for saying it. The 'we're-all-right' mentality.

'Bill,' I said mildly, 'I'm telling ya.' But he was determined to carry on as if nothing was happening. We finished with the LF at the end of that week and on Sunday saw a story in *The Mirror*: GANGSTERS NAIL MAN'S FOOT TO FLOOR. The story was written in such a way as to be as ambiguous as possible – perhaps they didn't have the proof. But they alluded to the Kray twins. And now everyone had to know something was up. Somebody was poking around.

Now Bill was as excited as me about who might be in the area. If it was in the papers it was as if he'd never disbelieved me in the first place. But he still didn't think it was Old Bill who had been in the car.

'Maybe they were reporters.' Yeah, all right, Bill. I got hold of Reggie.

'Look, it's getting a bit warm,' I said earnestly. 'I think it's on us here, you know. I don't feel comfortable. We gotta get out somehow. It's no use being sitting ducks.'

Reggie had an idea. 'I know a bloke who's got The Glenrae Hotel over at Finsbury Park.' I'd never heard of the hotel or Ted, its owner. I didn't even know how he knew him, but I didn't ever ask questions of the twins. Reggie said he would have a chat with this fella, 'see if he'll let us use the place for a bit.'

The Glenrae was generally quiet, mainly used by travelling businessmen passing by through London on the Seven Sisters Road. It was unremarkable, out of the way – the perfect hideaway. Ted was more than agreeable.

'If any of you want to meet any of your friends,' he said to Reggie. 'I can open up the bar downstairs for you.' There was quite a sizeable venue downstairs. Which was just as well. Within two weeks, our bolthole was the busiest club in London. This was the twins being discreet. They just couldn't help themselves. It was packed. They were turning people away and Ted was delighted. We might not be very secretive but he was earning a fortune. The regular Kray crowd liked to spend big. Once again, Ronnie and Reggie slipped comfortably into the role of mine hosts.

Reggie's wife Frances was supposed to come along with him one night but he turned up without her. He beckoned me over frantically and we slipped out of the bar so he could talk in private.

'What's the matter?' I asked.

'A strange thing,' he said. 'When I was getting ready tonight, there was a knock on the front door. I'd just heard a couple of bangs, like shots. I didn't take that much notice. And then there's a knock on the door. It was Jimmy Evans. And Jimmy said, "They've just shot Ginger Marks." I wanted to ask him more but he just went, "No, don't hang about, I gotta go." And that was it.'

Tommy Marks was shot in the street and his body taken away. Reggie was clearly a bit shaken up by the news. We had a meeting to investigate who might be behind the killing.

I said, 'Freddie Foreman's done that.' I was roundly disbelieved, though Charlie was despatched to ask Freddie himself. He was met with the expected denial, although Freddie did admit he was busily turning his own house upside down trying to find his diary. He was clearly trying to dispose of evidence.

Inevitably, the Old Bill steamed into The Glenrae just a few nights later. I wasn't there to see them checking up chimneys, looking under beds – they were after Marks's body. Poor old Ted wasn't so sure he'd got a good deal now.

But The Glenrae remained popular and the guests included the gay son of a baronet called Hew McCowan. He asked the twins if they would be interested in becoming his partners in a Soho nightclub he was setting up called The Hideaway. The venue was then owned by Gilbert France, who also ran the renowned restaurant Chez Victor in Wardour Street. Ronnie agreed and McCowan made a big mistake. He changed his mind and came back to tell an enraged Ronnie a couple of nights later – in front of everyone. McCowan was to be blanked from then on, just as journalist Tom Bryant had earlier fallen out with the twins over the 'axeman' story. We were all to glare at him to make him feel uncomfortable and clear off. In the end, though, McCowan was to have his revenge – and without lifting a finger.

A friend of Ronnie's called Teddy Smith was in McCowan's club one night and was thrown out for being too pissed and becoming a pest. Around the same time a TV crew was touring Soho trying to find people who'd been threatened by gangsters. When McCowan was asked, he jumped in and claimed that Teddy Smith was sent by Ronnie to demand a share of The Hideaway. The TV crew passed the report to the police. It was all they needed to arrest the twins.

At that time the Old Bill were going through a period of using Volkswagens, one of which I saw outside The Glenrae when I was going to pick up my car one day. It made a change from the Hillman Hunter. This time I was completely certain about identifying them – I'd seen the car's driver before. I immediately went to the nearest phonebox and called Ronnie.

'I'm not going to try and talk code in case you don't understand me,' I said urgently. 'There's Old Bill fucking everywhere! Now, *get out.* Old Bill everywhere. Don't hang about, I'm telling you.'

'Okay, Mick,' came the decidedly cool response.

'I'm not coming back, by the way,' I said. 'I'm going to get out of the way.'

Within a couple of days they were nicked. Next time I saw Ronnie Kray he was in Brixton Prison.

'Ron!' I said. 'I gave you that message. Why didn't you act on it?'

He looked unimpressed. 'Well. We came out that night and we looked around. We couldn't see anything and we said, "Oh, he's *mad*."' No wonder they got arrested. The pair of them were so short-sighted they wouldn't have seen anyone.

It was quite ironic – Hew McCowan's allegation was not at all true but that was the charge that put them on remand when there was no shortage of crimes they were guilty of. That wasn't an uncommon experience, though. The hardest thing of all was to defend yourself against the thing you haven't done. You can always think of an alibi when you know where you have to pretend not to have been and what you have to pretend you've never done. If you haven't got an answer at all you're going to look guilty. It was quite a few months before they managed to get themselves out of that.

I was with Charlie at Vallance Road one morning while the twins were away when the post came.

Opening a letter Charlie said, 'Listen to this, Mick. "Don't you care what happens to us, Charlie, or are you just a brainless cunt?"' Poor old Charlie, that is what he had to put up with.

At that moment there was a knock on the door. Some fella called Byrne turned up and said, 'Sorry, but I'm part of the conspiracy against you and your brothers. I know they didn't do it.'

And that was how we learned the truth. This fella wasn't someone we knew, but rather a friend of Hew McCowan, perhaps one of his boyfriends. The police had got him to make a statement and now he had thought better of it. We got straight on to George Devlin, the private detective who worked for Samson and Co, the solicitors. The twins' solicitor took a statement of what really happened but even then – such was feeling against the Krays – the jury was still hung. Lord Boothby used parliamentary privilege to demand of the government whether they intended to keep the twins inside for ever. It was only when the case went to retrial that it was at last thrown out by the judge. Writers would later make much more of the story, but the real facts of the Krays' and McCowan affair were really that straightforward.

Gilbert France, who knew the twins, suggested they take over The Hideaway.

'I don't want McCowan in there now,' he told them. 'After all these problems he's caused for you – it's ridiculous.'

The club was reopened as El Morocco, after a famous New York venue, but as with everything with the twins, it was all smoke and mirrors. It would subsequently be claimed by those who bought into the Krays' myths that they bought the place. In truth, no money had changed hands and suddenly they fronted up a big nightclub. The Krays had club business cards printed for themselves and Freddie Foreman.

I thought this was taking the piss out of the police. The Krays thought they didn't need to learn any lessons, but the coppers took careful note of how their case collapsed. For so long the police had been used to swooping on anyone they wanted, like in the Longfleet robbery when those two innocent men, Bill C and Bill S, were arrested. The police nailed them with whatever circumstantial evidence they could find. It was an easy result and the case didn't need to be that tight. But even the police could see that the same approach didn't work with the Krays. They couldn't take them down on a whisper.

Now the twins were drawing attention to the police's failures. In beating the case, the twins had, in effect, denied they had anything to do with the club. And then they took it over with maximum publicity, their guests including the likes of comedian Frankie Howerd. They were showing nothing less than open contempt for the police. I thought there was no need for antagonising the Old Bill like that. I didn't want my name on that business card and I didn't even consider going to the opening night. Yes, it was a glitzy affair which was widely reported by the media, but who was outside the entrance, taking photos of everyone as they arrived? Scotland Yard's finest, Nipper Read, the man who would achieve fame by bringing down the Krays. This was where he started his work.

I even told Reggie of my fears.

'We've got to step back a bit. We're too much on show all the time. We've got these big meets and loads of people turn up. You have a pub full of people on the meet for no reason.'

'Yeah, right, we'll talk about that,' he said. When he got back to me it was to say they were going to 'decentralise'. That was the first time I heard the term. Somebody must have given them that one. He said that the next meet would be in Walthamstow, a few miles further out. That was the extent of the changes.

The El Morocco didn't last very long. I don't know why, as I wasn't involved with it, but I think there were financial reasons behind its closure. During its relatively brief life, Ronnie introduced me to the psychiatrist responsible for his treatment and medication. He was a guest one night.

'He's Dr Klein,' said Ronnie, 'from the London hospital. He's very upset. In a right state. He was telling me he's just come back from Switzerland. He went out there with a girl – this fella's much older – and she committed suicide out there. He's come back, Dr Klein, and he's all depressed so I sent him over a bottle of champagne. That'll straighten him out – he'll be all right, now. You watch.'

The story sounded terrifying but Ronnie's attitude was very self-satisfied. He was essentially telling me how clever he was, having sorted out his psychiatrist's problems for him.

Dr Klein himself didn't have quite such an easy going view of his client. Charlie Kray told me what Klein said about Ronnie.

'If he ever has a drink,' said Klein, 'I don't want to be around. I won't be responsible for that – I'll wash my hands of the whole matter.'

I don't think Charlie told him that Ronnie's record for drinking was 28 brown ales straight off in The Double R. Big Pat kept the bottles for posterity – equivalent to something like 14 pints in one sitting.

In The Double R having a drink with Ossie, Dickie Moughton and Reggie talking with Tommy McGoven, British Lightweight Title Contender.

Out celebrating down The Astor with (l to r) Terry Spinks, Sammy McCarthy and a guy named Dodger.

(l to r) Teddy Smith, myself, Johnny Davis, Reggie, Freddie Mills, Ronnie, Dicky Morgan and Sammy Lederman in Freddie Mills' Nite Spot.

(l to r) Harry Abrahams, Bill Collis, Jacky Reynolds, Wolfy
Gerber, Georgie Woods, Big Pat's wife, Big Pat, Old Charlie,
Buster Osbourne, Limehouse Willy, Alby Korsher, Billy
Donovan, myself at Big Pat's wedding

Dolly, Ronnie, Nobby Clarke, Barbara Windsor and Lita Rosa
suround Sonny Liston.

(l to r) Bobby Ramsey, Henry Simonds, Ronnie, Sonny Liston
and myself leaving The Cambridge Rooms.

Ronnie objects to an outsider trying to shake hands with
Sonny Liston.

Liston signs a fan's autograph watched by an admiring Dolly Kray.

Ronnie with the love of his life Bobby Buckley.

From back left: Buller Ward, Freddie Foreman, Charlie, Albert Donaghue, Billy Donovan, Reggie, Dicky Moughton,Terry Allen ex-world flyweight champion, Ronnie, Red Face Tommy, Old Steff, Big Pat Connolly, Ossie, Harry Coshaw. Front row: Freddie Cavanagh, Eddie Flowers, Old Charlie, myself, BBBC official.

102

Billy Hill at home

In Freddie Mills' Nite Spot, myself, Reggie, Frances, Peter and Freddie Mills.

Johnny Davies, Nobby Clark, Dolly Kray, myself with Lenny Peters, Bobby Ramsey, Big Pat, Terry O'Brien, Ronnie, Sonny Liston and Reggie.

A tribute evening to the great Ted "Kid" Lewis who had 303 pro fights. From left: Reggie, Sulky, Ronnie, Ronnie Gill, George Last, Ted 'Kid' Lewis, myself, Limehouse Willy, Terry Spinks, Charlie, Nobby Clarke, Billy Exley, Joe Abrahams, Dave Simonds, Andrew Ray (kneeling)

In The Dolce Vita, Newcastle - (from left to right) myself, Billy Daniels, Reggie, Johnny Squib, Johnny Davies, a guy called Peter, Eric Mason and Ronnie.

Johnny Squib, Charlie, Ronnie, Dukey Osbourne, Johnny Davies, Sammy Lederman, Bobby Ramsey, Eddie Pucci - Mafia man and Frank Sinatra's bodyguard, Reggie, Shirley Bassey and Jimmy Clark of the Clark Brothers.

Sammy Lederman, Charlie, Dolly, Noel Harrison, Reggie, Myself, Lita Rosa, Ronnie, Barbara Windsor and Ronald Fraser.

Larry Gains - British Empire (Commonwealth) heavyweight
champion, Ronnie and Johnny Davies with the twins' racehorse
Solway Cross.

Chapter Eight

Sticking the Krays Up

The Kentucky Club was in Mile End Road and it was almost empty. Reggie walked over to the young man and hit him right on the chin. Then he booted him repeatedly. Nobody did anything. I feel a bit ashamed about that. There were just a few of us still there that night, Freddie Foreman too, among others. But nobody raised a finger. The object of Reggie's rage was a mental health nurse from Scotland. Having been restrained in secure institutions, Ronnie was winding up his brother by painting the man as a screw in a prison.

The lad was there with Stanley Crowther, an ex-barrister, gay, alcoholic wreck, who would give evidence against the twins in the end – and I didn't blame him. He was like a seedy old lawyer character in a film noir, but not a bad old boy really. It was the long firm he fronted for the twins out of Great Eastern Street which had been scuppered when Ronnie took the money early. When he visited the club with the nurse, I couldn't see at first that either of them had done anything wrong, but it became clear that somehow disrespect had been shown and that in itself wasn't unusual. There was no predicting when they might take offence.

At the end of the night, Reggie said to Stanley's friend, 'Don't let Stanley shoot off, will you? I wanna have a word with him.'

Reggie was in full cunning mode. He made it sound innocent enough and Stanley was duly persuaded to hang about when in fact, it was his friend who was in trouble.

It was a vile incident and I've since come to feel even worse about it as I've had experience myself of dealing with people

109

who have been in the mental health system. Those nurses can be really good and although I thought the victim that night wasn't permanently injured – I certainly hope not – he undeniably took a right belting.

It was the same with Sonny – that fella I'd first met back in the Aldgate warehouse days. Sonny was retired by then and his offence was to be patronising, putting his arm around Reggie and assuring him that if there was 'ever anything you want me to do' he would. Reggie broke his jaw. More than anything, it was touching that Reggie couldn't stand. I seemed to get away with it – I've got a photo of myself with my arm draped over Reggie's shoulder with a few other mates at a club up north. Most people found themselves sitting on the floor if they dared touch his personage. It was a bit like getting familiar with the Queen.

Fans of the Krays either never got to hear of those outbursts or they chose to ignore them. The famous and the successful hung on their every word in a way that never sat easily with me. Director Joan Littlewood was always at The Kentucky with her thespian chums. She had been working down the road at the Theatre Royal Stratford and had come to be such a big admirer of the twins that she once confided to me she wanted to make a film about them. A fictionalised account with her own choice of actors.

The slightly pock-marked face of Chuck Sewell was another regular sight at the club. He was an actor, but not as well known as Victor Spinetti, another permanent fixture. Not only was he always at the club, but he made it into the eventual Krays' film that was, unfortunately, not made by Joan Littlewood. She would have done a better job. I hated the way that movie turned out and the twins didn't like it either.

But they loved having the celebrities around and were thrilled to be invited to the premiere of *Sparrows Can't Sing* at the ABC, a cinema which stood opposite The Kentucky. I usually blanked all of those showbiz events. They were a real bore. Whenever the stars were around the conversation would always have to be about the twins. That was all any of them were interested in. Ronnie and Reggie were happy to play along. That night they were the only ones done up in dinner suits, standing out from everyone else with their bow ties. A friend of mine whispered to me, 'I can't wait to see if one of them stars thinks Ronnie's a waiter and asks him to get a drink.'

I hated all the hero worship you heard from the twins' famous friends. 'Wonderful fellows, aren't they!', 'They give a fortune to charity!' Totally untrue. They didn't give a fucking penny to charity! The most charitable they'd get would be to send someone down a long firm and get the people running it to order a television. They'd then donate whatever they fraudulently obtained to some old folks' home in a blaze of publicity. It was very cynical. I just didn't like the way famous people lapped up the fakery. The stars themselves were okay, but I just didn't feel comfortable in that world.

Other villains were just as desperate to be seen with the Krays. It seems that anyone who ever met the twins has sold their story. One of the worst offenders is Lenny Hamilton, the little weasel. He is always sticking himself up as a jewel thief, although to me he's always seemed more like the type to be a minicab driver. In the words of the old saying, 'he lies faster than a horse can trot'. He was never anything, but it's true he did get on the wrong side of the twins. Ronnie tortured him with a red hot steel used for sharpening knives. Lenny tried to make more out of it, saying that Ronnie went after him. Ronnie didn't care about him – the truth was that Lenny made a nuisance of himself and put himself squarely in Ronnie's sights.

Lenny phoned late one night to tell Ronnie that he'd just beaten up the son of Buller Ward – one of those fellas who'd come with me on the Paris trip. Lenny pleaded for Ronnie not to get involved and asked if he could meet to talk to him about it. It was a very cheeky request. Ronnie wouldn't normally have got involved and he didn't know Lenny anyway. Now he was fuming.

Ronnie arranged the meet at Esmeralda's Barn, but kept Reggie out of it, knowing his slightly wiser brother wouldn't have wanted to get them involved with anything so basically trivial. At The Barn, Hamilton was held down in a chair while Ronnie scorched his face and blinded him in one eye. Ever since then, the media has been happy to repeat Hamilton's version of events – that Ronnie got involved on behalf of Buller Ward. It suits everyone to keep the legends alive.

Lenny Hamilton was himself one of a little crew led by a fella named Harry Abrahams. They were outraged by Lenny's punishment. Harry operated out of The Kentucky with Norman Winters, Bunny Harris, Billy Thomas – a nice guy from Hoxton – and Albert Donaghue, known to all of us as Albert Barry. Harry Abrahams went on to get five years for a robbery which got Albert three years. I got on well with most of them. Though when Harry said, 'We've had enough of this. We're going to do Ronnie,' I thought, thanks for telling me! I need to know that, don't I? But I also knew that once he'd told me, he wouldn't really go through with it. The rest of them made a bit of a fuss about it, but it was mainly Harry who complained the loudest. He gave it plenty of verbal.

Unfortunately, Ronnie got to hear something of what was going on and he asked Harry's mob to meet him at Vallance Road. Harry later filled me in.

'We've settled it,' he said. 'Ronnie was sitting there with his bull terrier, just on his own.'

This was typical Ronnie. He would enjoy the fact that he was the lone desperado facing down the enemy. It bought out his theatrical side. But he hadn't forgotten what they planned to do and called me in to ask me about it. At that time Ronnie lived at 66 Cedra Court, a nice block of flats in Stamford Hill. A tenor recital was playing when I arrived.

'Listen to this music,' he said. 'It's very good.'

'Is that Gigli?' I asked, 'or Mario Lanza?'

Without a hint of a smile he said, 'Harry Secombe.'

Ronnie said he had been to Steeple Bay. Just hearing that made me shudder. It was the most boring place on earth, a caravan site in Essex on the Blackwater estuary near Maldon. The Krays used to go there, big time, for weekends away. I couldn't think of anything worse – you'd send me there as some kind of punishment. Ronnie said he hadn't heard the full story but just knew that there was a plan to shoot him. Did I know anything?

I said, 'No. I don't know anything about that, Ron.'

'Well, I thought I'd ask you because you'd know.' He wasn't sounding threatening and he seemed convinced that I hadn't heard anything.

It was not wise to bother the Krays unless you really needed to. Boxing promoter Mickey Duff was another one who got in touch when perhaps he would have been better off just getting on with things. Reggie passed on the message that Duff had phoned and although I wasn't there for the conversation, what he had apparently said made everyone extremely tense.

I'd first seen Mickey Duff when he was the matchmaker at Mile End Arena when I was 13. He was now telling Reggie he'd got a licence to open what he called The Anglo-American Sporting Club in the Park Lane Hilton and – this was the killer – 'Would you mind not coming?' Not very tactful. 'We don't want any faces there because we're on a trial and we may not get renewed.'

Duff didn't know the twins – and if he had he probably wouldn't have asked for a favour like that. If he hadn't mentioned it they probably wouldn't have thought of going anyway. Now they had been specifically de-invited and everyone was very upset.

The story that has since been well documented is that the Krays sent Duff four dead rats. It was a chilling message – though not quite what it seemed. They'd sent someone down the pet shop but he came back with four gerbils. Still, who could tell the difference once they had been killed and spent a couple of days in the post? It was a typical gesture by the twins. Nothing was what it seemed with them – even dead rats.

The twins followed up with a bomb hoax. They nominated Dukey Osbourne to call up during the next of Duff's boxing promotions at the Hilton. Duke proudly reported back down the pub that he'd done it and that he'd made himself sound suitably manic.

'There's a bomb under the ring, evacuate the building!' he said, showing off the theatrical gasps he'd used during the call. 'Evacuate! I can't say more!'

But there were no reports from anyone connected to the promotion, much less in the press. Discreet inquiries from our side followed. It turned out that Duff had been hosting some kind of ladies' night – there wasn't a fight and they hadn't even set up a ring. Mickey Duff remained entirely unintimidated.

If the Krays always came off worse in these kinds of situations it was because at heart they were afraid of straight people. That was behind all that hot-headed belligerence and it was the reason they never planned properly. They were scared. That's why they didn't set out to intimidate anyone in the straight world. They gave them a right miss. They spectacularly misjudged Mickey Duff who, if he was as ruthless and hard-nosed as you needed to be to succeed as a boxing promoter, wasn't in their world. And they knew it.

You were only at risk if they thought you were like them. It didn't matter if you weren't exactly a criminal, even if you were straight and you somehow ended up doing business with them then that made you fair game. I saw people getting themselves into trouble and I often stepped in to stop them making a fatal mistake. I must have saved three or four lives when I was around the twins. I mean that literally; I stopped people from being killed, usually over nothing.

There was the time a fella called Tom Clegg turned up at Vallance Road claiming to be a messenger. He was a big bloke, with a scar on his face, though he wasn't a criminal. I didn't know him and I never ran into him again.

'I've come to speak to you on behalf of Joe Sullivan, a friend of mine in Southsea, Portsmouth,' he said. 'He's afraid. He's been told he's made a terrible mistake and he's liable to be killed by you.'

It was a complicated plot and it sounded like Joe Sullivan had got himself into a big mess. He owned a very large scrapyard called Southern Counties Metals and had dealings with a fella named Ronnie Atrill from Brighton. Atrill got him to put up money for some crooked scheme and then, to all intents and purposes, disappeared.

An angry Sullivan commissioned four fellas to sort him out – Ronnie Moore, Ronnie Molloy, Jimmy Tibbs Sr, known by everyone as Big Jim, and Billy Smith. When they reported back to Joe Sullivan the news wasn't good.

'We've got a terrible problem,' they told Joe. 'We've tuned him up, we've slashed him, but he was meant to front a long firm for the Kray twins. Now they're after us. We need some money to square the Krays otherwise it's all going to come back to you, Joe, because in their eyes you're the instigator.'

This was news in Vallance Road and for good reason – Atrill had conspired with the four men sent after him. The Krays were never involved at all. The four men had come up with the story to frighten Sullivan while Atrill kept out of the way.

We went off to talk about what to do. Ronnie was furious that they had bought his name into a fabricated story, essentially over nothing. I tried to calm things down, saying, 'I'll go down and see this Joe Sullivan.'

I went to Southern Counties Metals with my men Tommy Brown and Teddy Machin, someone I would later have a major falling out with. We managed to sort things out with Sullivan. The nearest he came to a clump was when he said to Tommy Brown, 'You're a travelling man ain't you, mush?' Both of them were gypsy stock.

'What?' asked Tommy.

'Fancy a bit of hotchi pie?' he said mockingly.

Hotchi was hedgehog and although Sullivan was only taking the piss, Tommy didn't see the funny side and I had to pull him back. But there wasn't really an atmosphere by that point. I'd assured Sullivan that although the Krays had been told about this local dispute, there wasn't really anything to worry about.

'This will go no further,' I had promised Joe Sullivan, who I later became friends with. 'I just want to know who helped you out.' I was back in Vallance Road the same day to confirm the four names with the twins.

'Make them meet with me over Johnny Hutton's,' roared Ronnie.

Hutton's was a car site over in Walthamstow where Ronnie had once already shot somebody in the leg after they complained about the motor they bought off him. Unwisely, the purchaser told him, 'This car is no good,' provoking the display of Ronnie's unorthodox approach to customer satisfaction. But even that violent outburst was nothing compared to how angry he seemed to be over Atrill's men.

When the twins lost it, they really lost it. I knew the signs. They would get worked up and stand, facing, angrily searching one another, patting each other down, wanting to be sure the other one wasn't about to do anything without warning. Mainly this was Reggie checking out what his madder brother might be carrying. Interrogating one another – 'All right, Ron, what you got there? What you got there?'

Ronnie's style was to keep a gun hidden because he just didn't want to hear reason. He might even know deep down that taking someone out might not always be the best move but he wasn't going to listen. If he wanted to do it and he felt it was right, that was enough. He wouldn't even tell his brother and that was why they were now virtually squaring up, each pushing the other to greater fury. It was a terrifying sight. They were ready to head to Hutton's place immediately.

The worst possible thing you could do to the Krays was stick their name up. That was all they had. This was the corporate name being used on inferior goods and passed off as the real thing. As I knew, there were benefits to knowing the Krays. If you used their name and you were for real, you could be assured of getting the best of everything. And so it was true that they needed to protect their name – but they just didn't have any sense of proportion. They were immediately ready to kill.

I knew I couldn't do anything to calm them down, but I didn't allow myself to get swept up in their madness. Ronnie in particular would only get more violent at any attempt at rational discussion. It would have been fatal to have given any hint that I thought this might be anything less than a brilliant plan. There had to be another way. This wasn't being brave, it just made more sense. To be honest, the worst people around the twins were the yes-men. They were the real killers. They made Ronnie feel like Superman and that there was nothing he couldn't do. He hardly needed convincing of that at the best of times. That was what brought the twins down in the end.

You had to know when to come back with a hard and effective response to avoid looking weak but at the same time try not to go along with their tendency for overkill. They were always over the top. When they attacked the twins never bothered to mask up. The positive side effect was that if they were after you and you managed to avoid them for a bit they would probably forget after a while, unless you kept on doing whatever it was they had taken against. They didn't know how to track people down and they didn't have the strategy to maintain a campaign.

The twins got a long way on their natural charisma alone. It blinded many to what should have been obvious faults – their lack of intelligence, organisational ability and common sense. They looked the part and they had those famous good manners. Don't underestimate how far that gets you, even in the underworld, particularly when you're usually dealing with brainless muscle and chancers. I knew what was behind their image. If the time came for me to break off relations with them I could be secure in the knowledge that they'd never be able find me without help. I might have been working with the Krays, but I'm not sure I ever really respected them. Perhaps I was getting to know them too well.

When it came to dealing with the men who used the Kray name, I was able to appeal to both brothers. There was one thing that always got their attention.

'Will you leave this to me?' I said. 'I'll probably be able to make an earner of it.' The magic words. They didn't have that much of an effect on Ronnie, but Reggie went my way.

He said, 'Okay,' and I headed to Canning Town that same night. I met with Big Jim Tibbs in a pub and all I needed to do was be honest.

I never thought there was any point in going in heavy-handed. Partly this was because the news that the Kray brothers were irritated was in itself an effective threat, as I had found when I eventually spoke to Atrill. But I found that people reacted well if I offered to help them out.

'Listen, I've come to do you a favour,' I said and advised my terrified audience how to deal with their major problem. 'It's a tumble. The twins know it was you. The best thing to do is return it or give me the money and you won't hear no more about it.'

I practised a kind of reverse intimidation.

'I'm not going to set about you,' I said. 'I'm just going to go if you're not interested.'

The implication was always very clear. The next visit would be from the twins themselves and any sane person would do anything to avoid that. My approach never failed. The most resistance I got was from those who reckoned themselves and would give me a bit of chat. They thought they could talk their way out of it but they soon sobered up when they realised how serious I was.

Big Jim Tibbs was not going to give me any trouble. He knew who he was dealing with when it came to the Krays, having been charged with and acquitted of murder himself, along with Georgie Woods, Teddy Robbins and Don Mooney of the Queen's Road mob. Big Jim was a scrap metal dealer with a reputation of his own.

He had three sons who were also well known and I would later have a major feud with them. At this time their father was worried about Ronnie and Reggie coming to get him. Now Big Jim's worst fears seemed about to be realised. He believed me immediately. I told him about the money and laid out the options for him – which weren't exactly plentiful. Jim didn't blink when I told him how much cash he'd need to give me. He said precisely eight words in response.

'God! Can I go and get it now?'

'Yeah,' I said, 'go on, then.'

I didn't need to wait long. The story was the same with each of the conspirators. I don't even remember how much money they gave me, but it wasn't insignificant. It would have been something like 500 quid – and from each, not in total. It was a sort of fine. Here was the real protection money, if the papers cared to look for it, but, of course, they'd never get to hear of it. But these men were more easily frightened than any owner of a legitimate small business.

Most of the money went back to the Krays, though I knew I'd be able hang on to some of it. That was how I earned money when I wasn't on the long firms. They would ask me to do something for them and it was just simply understood that if the money came through me, some of it was going stick to me. I didn't need to hide that – the twins would know how much I took.

I also knew that if we were splitting the proceeds, it would be three ways – not just between the twins and me, 50/50, but between me, Ronnie and Reggie. Three ways. Other people didn't get such a good deal. Someone might ask if he could use the Krays' name to do some work and agree to a split without waiting to specify who got what until the job was done.

The fella who did all the work would sit in Vallance Road in dismay as the money was divided between him and Reggie, Ronnie – and Charlie. Four ways. The Krays had evolved a clever system, particularly considering they had little formal education. That was 75% for the loan of their name. Most of their associates were too stupid to spot how badly they had come off. Some might think that wasn't a bad deal and others might disagree but all would see the wisdom in not saying so. That was standard practice and Jimmy

Tibbs Sr that night at the pub knew that making his offering saved him from – at best – a severe beating. Perhaps much worse. And it wasn't the last time I would be thrown together with him. Later on, as you'll see, he played a major role in my life.

Chapter Nine

LIFE SAVER

I stood at the front door and I spoke clearly and deliberately. I kept completely still and I didn't raise my voice.

The man was a right Jack the Lad until I said, 'You were seen with Reggie Kray's bird the other night.' I knew the words would have an effect on him, but I hadn't expected him, almost in one movement, to leap backwards and slam the door in my face. The letterbox opened and a pair of terrified eyes peered at me.

I said, 'Open the door.'

'No! Talk to me through this,' he shouted. 'I don't care if my wife hears!'

'Open the fucking door!'

He was scared, but he did it. I saw he was crying and shaking. Snot dribbled down over his mouth. He pleaded and begged indistinctly. I kept my own voice level and spoke as kindly as I could. There was no need to be any heavier.

'It's nearly on you,' I said. 'Behave yourself in future.'

Reggie had told me of his suspicions the night before in The Grave Maurice. He was engaged to Frances and he was worried.

'Mick, I've got something I must talk to you about,' he said. 'I was outside her house the other night, sitting in the car and watching. A fella came home with her very late at night and dropped her off. I took his car number down and I HPI'd it.'

He was referring to doing a hire purchase investigation, something that was carried out by car dealers as a routine check on the details of potential buyers. Johnny Hutton, who owned the Walthamstow firm used by the Krays, had run the enquiry for him.

'I've got his address,' said Reggie, 'and I wanna do him.'

It would have been easy to go along with this but I didn't want to cause unnecessary trouble and I just felt there was something here that I thought could be done differently. I knew right away why Reggie had come to me, because he was terrified the Colonel would have found out and driven him mad, the main thing for me was to give him a get out.

'Hold tight now, Reg,' I said. 'I'll sort it out. Leave it to me, okay?' And Reggie let me get on with it.

Perhaps, deep down, he wanted only to know that Frances wasn't playing around. If there was a way I could get him out of it with his own dignity intact it had to be worth trying. But I had no real idea of what I was going to do. I needed this particular job like a hole in the head and come closing time I was pretty irritated by being caught up in Reggie's tangled life again. I went home and to bed.

I was woken at about 5.00 am by a knocking on the window. I didn't connect it with the conversation in the pub, not least because I lived in Upton Park at the time, a long way from Reggie. But there he was, staring in at me when I pulled back the curtain. Reggie! What now? I left the house to talk with him outside.

'I can't sleep!' he said. 'Can we do that today?'

It all came flooding back. I knew what he meant – he wanted to go and find this fella who had been with Frances.

'All right, Reg, calm down,' I said. 'What's his address?'

Southern Road, Plaistow. I stalled, telling Reggie that we couldn't do anything at this time of night. To kill time we went for an aimless drive around for a couple of hours. Reggie was still agitated, but at least I was more in control now. We weren't just tearing off on instinct. We finished up at Stevie Tucker's house. He was a good few years older than me, but a reliable friend – he still is and he's in his 80s now – and I knew I could leave Reggie there out of harm's way with Stevie's wife, Lou.

Reggie seemed relieved that he didn't need to go himself. His own way of dealing with things would have been less direct than his brother but just as violent in the end. If Reggie was going to chin you, he would often first compliment you on your tie or shirt to put you at ease and to make sure he got the first punch in, you had no chance. The newspapers had it that Reggie would offer someone a smoke and, as they lit it, would then chin them: the 'cigarette punch'. All very dramatic. He might have done it once, but what a lot of cobblers.

Some time after half eight, Stevie drove me in his own car to an unremarkable terraced house not that far away. The small front garden had a gate and the fella, a car dealer, eventually answered my knock on the door, half-asleep, no shirt.

'Yes, mate? Whaddya want?'

I stood on the pavement, not opening the gate.

'I want a word with you,' I said. 'And I don't want your wife to hear.' He looked annoyed as he stepped into the garden, pulling the door to slightly behind him.

'What? Whaddya want?'

And we had the exchange that ended up with him cowering indoors and weeping. Stevie Tucker saw it all, killing himself laughing in the car, and I joined in as we drove back to report to Reggie. He was anxiously waiting to hear what had happened.

I had my story straight.

'Frances is a friend of a daughter of that fella. So what's happened is, he's gone, "If you're going home, I'll drop you off." They were out together, that's what it was. You've got it all wrong, Reg!'

Reggie really did sigh with relief. But he looked troubled.

'Dear, oh dear,' he said. 'Mick, she ain't been at it or anything like that, has she?'

'Oh, shut up, Reg,' I said. 'For fuck's sake! Course she ain't! What you on about? I just told you!'

And that was the end of it. But the car dealer was very lucky it was me and not one of Reggie's other mates. And the fella knew it. I did a bit of research on him afterwards just in case it might turn out to be useful. His name was Levy. But – not surprisingly – we never heard from Mr Levy again and he never went near Frances.

Frances had first come on the scene when she was just 16. I would sometimes give her a lift home from Vallance Road. She was attractive, but her role was simply to be arm candy for Reggie. She had to look the part and be everything for him. She was not welcome as far as Ronnie was concerned. With the one exception of the twins' mother, Ronnie thought women were, in general, vile, dirty creatures, but he particularly loathed Frances. She came between the brothers. It has been suggested that the twins had a sexual relationship, which couldn't be further from the truth, but Ronnie did see the end of their partnership in Frances and never lost an opportunity to get at her.

He fired me one of his loaded questions one day.

'What do you think of his bird, Mick?' It was hard enough to answer at the best of times, but particularly tough as Reggie was also there. I tried to be as neutral as possible, but he wouldn't let it go.

'Ain't she got horrible legs?' It was one of those occasions when I couldn't do more than say as little as possible, wait for the punches to start flying and remove myself from the increasingly tense situation as politely but quickly as I could.

Frances's admirer wasn't the only life I had a hand in preserving. There was also Dickie Bennett, a singer and completely straight. Somehow he had ended up in the twins' orbit and they had decided they were going to manage him. This sort of thing was always happening – no doubt some local businessman character knew Dickie and thought he could help him out with his career and get in with the twins if he introduced them. A nice theory, but it was harder to picture a less likely match. Slim, lively and wearing a pork-pie hat, Dickie was every inch the Sinatra-esque crooner. There was no way he belonged in the world of the twins and it was small wonder that he almost ended up at the bottom of the Thames.

Reggie more or less ordered me to look after Dickie. Ronnie was against him from the start. But they wanted me to take him to a solicitor called Ellis Lincoln who worked out of the City. Dickie was a nice little chap and we got on all right, though I knew as little as the twins about music management. The solicitor, very professional, very well spoken, listened closely.

'Right,' he said to Dickie. 'I'll give you some advice. Don't have anything to do with this. Find yourself a sensible manager.'

It was indeed ridiculous. The twins barely knew how to run their own career. And Ronnie didn't even believe in Dickie. So when I told them what happened they weren't too bothered. And anyway, Dickie had a booking in a club in Newcastle called La Dolce Vita. Would I take him up there? Again, it was an order rather than a request. I knew there was no money involved in this and it would be hard to see how I could make any unless Dickie hit the big time with them.

At least we had fun up north for a few days. Dickie sang and performed while I enjoyed what turned out to be one of the most impressive clubs I'd ever seen. The early '60s were just the start of the era of big clubs owned by the likes of the Bailey brothers. There were photos of Dickie Bennett up in town and the three Kaye sisters. Coincidentally, I had to go up again to visit someone in Durham jail and dropped by the club again. Owner Marcus Levy was in that night and remembered me from before.

'How you going?' I asked. 'All right?'

'Listen,' he said. 'Everything's on me tonight. Free. You speak a bit of Yiddish?'

'Yeah.'

'We was in schtuck,' he said.

The club was massive and I couldn't see how they had trouble with a venue that size. All Marcus added was, 'And I just got out of it. Order what you like, have what you want. It's all down to me and the best of luck to you.'

The friend I was with was amazed by the reception – but that was just how it was at the time. It transpired on that very day Marcus had finalised the sale of the club to the Bailey brothers.

When I told the twins how enjoyable the visit was, they arranged a return with a full complement of Kray associates and another singer, Billy Daniels, who did *That Old Black Magic*. This excursion became something of a legend thanks to media reports, which painted it as the Krays attempting to take over Newcastle and failing. It was nothing of the kind and the idea itself, if you thought about it, was total nonsense. You can't go to a town and take it over as if it was a fast-food franchise. Even the great Machiavelli, the fifteenth-century Italian schemer, always said you had to live somewhere to know how it works and to run it. He had a point. We were really in the north for little more than an excuse for a works' outing.

Ronnie came with his gun-keeper, Johnny Davies, who had too much to drink one night and was sick in little piles all the way to his room, almost like a trail. Along the corridor, by the door, inside the room. Davies was sharing the room with his boss and promptly went to sleep. The hotel staff, meanwhile, were beginning an investigation which they probably wished they hadn't bothered with when they saw what awaited them behind Ronnie and Johnny's door. More sick by Johnny's bed, Johnny fast asleep and Ronnie in bed with the bell hop.

Ronnie had much less fun whenever Dickie Bennett was around and would be skulking and growling about how the idea of managing him was a complete waste of time. He was in a depressive mood. You could tell by his eyebrows. Ronnie's eyebrows would come down and knit together when he was bad and then it was best to leave him alone. He only responded to medication when he was like that. I knew it, but I have to admit I then made a tricky situation worse.

Dickie had committed some minor misdemeanour or looked the wrong way, or something, in the club and now Reggie also commented, 'Look at him!' in disgust.

My mistake was simply to express some level of agreement with whatever trivial point was being made. It was a fine line – if I stuck up for Dickie I could have made things worse.

I said, 'Yeah, Reg. Some people mistake kindness for weakness.'

It was a throwaway line, but Reggie said, 'Do they? Right. I'll show him.' With that he went over to Dickie. 'I want you to come somewhere with me,' he said.

The three of us, along with Johnny Squibb, got in the car and Reggie was to the point.

'Right, you're going in the river.'

Poor little Dickie Bennett was terrified, understandably, and yet for me there was something undeniably funny about finding myself in yet another mad scene straight out of a Hollywood gangster film. For no reason at all.

Reggie, though, was deadly serious and there was every chance that this could go badly wrong. If we said, 'No, you can't do that, Reg,' I knew that would be signing Dickie's death warrant. All we could do was keep driving around and wait for him to calm down.

We were in the car for an hour or more. We kept cool, brought up other subjects of conversation and generally tried to divert Reggie's thoughts. There would be no financial reward in Dickie dying, we suggested, no reputation to be gained for the Krays. We soothed, we were practical and we raised sensible considerations.

Gradually the danger faded as we turned from one street into another. It helped that Johnny Squibb was on my side and was a very old and trusted friend of Reggie.

Eventually I got the chance when we were pulled up to say to Dickie, 'Go on, have it away.'

I advised him to get out of sight and he took me very literally and went to America. I didn't blame him. Having survived the twins, I heard years later that he went on to do well in Las Vegas.

Chapter Ten

Billy Hill and the Unione Corse v the Krays

The twins were beginning to get on my nerves. Both of them were pissed all the time and there seemed to be more idiots around them every day. More of those inexperienced mugs who were attracted by the lifestyle. It wasn't like Freddie Foreman's lot – he had heavy-duty bank robbers around him who you wouldn't want to tangle with. The presence of lightweights with the Krays wasn't anything new, it just seemed there was more stupidity around than ever before. The twins were going nowhere.

After a while I began to get the message. Their hearts weren't in it and they just didn't seem to care. I'd still go out with Reggie though, though it did all feel a bit aimless. Esmeralda's Barn had also run its course when they offered the club to me. The venue was managed by their Uncle Alf and they owed a fortune in income tax on the limited company which was responsible for it.

'We'll sell you the company on paper,' they said. 'You'll owe the tax and there might be something you can do with the outfit.'

They were thinking I might swindle someone into investing in it. They didn't much care – they just wanted to know if it was of any use.

The liabilities didn't bother them.

'I don't pay tax – I'm a lunatic,' Ronnie would say.

I was similarly unmoved.

'Yeah,' I said without hesitation. What difference did it make? I didn't have bank accounts and there was no official trail leading to me. I needed only to duck and the tax would miss me. What could the Inland Revenue get off me? As far as the authorities were concerned, I didn't exist. But that was about all the deal had going for it. I had never been a gambler and you really needed to know the games to make a success of a den like Esmeralda's. You had to stick yourself up as a target for the other punters to aim at. It just wasn't my scene.

I thought it would be nice to have a place in Belgravia, even if I only managed to hold on to it for a fortnight. With that attitude it was hardly surprising that I didn't do much with the place. I took a couple of the waitresses out for dinner – that was about as far as it went. The biggest impact the place had on me was when I was eventually arrested along with the Krays and then the police didn't half grill me about having been in charge of The Barn.

The club limped on for a time but it had been over as a destination before the Krays handed it on. And when a club's over, it's over. It might be open but if the crowd have moved on, you can't bring it back to life. The twins wouldn't have handed it to me if there was still any mileage in it.

Reggie had half a mind to help me make something of The Barn. One night not long after I became the owner, I went out with him and Coxie, who was a very good friend and a very tough guy. We were visiting various venues when Reggie was seized upon the idea of checking out a hot venue, The 21 Club – in the house once owned by Lord Chesterfield in Chesterfield Gardens. It was the epitome of a Mayfair casino down to the liveried doormen, who barred entry, even to the famous Reginald Kray. We weren't members and there were no exceptions. Soon Reggie's famous left hook came over and the offending member of staff went down. His colleagues came out and a bit of a free-for-all started in the immaculate entrance to The 21. But in the way of those things, and there were many of them then, it was soon over and we took our custom to elsewhere, to The Astor.

We got inside without any trouble this time and – at last – we saw a friendly face. A fella named Patsy Murphy.

'How are you?' said Reggie. 'I've got Mick with me here, he's taken over The Barn. I don't know if there's anything you could do with these guys?'

It was all rather vague and I wondered what was on Reggie's mind. Probably no big scheme. Patsy was often to be seen in the casinos in the West End, he always had a few quid and he knew Billy Hill, whose influence in Mayfair was still very powerful. Billy had interests in gambling, from card games – which he loved – to betting shops all over that area of London. I guess Reggie knew it wasn't going well for me. Having passed Esmeralda's on, he was looking for any kind of inspiration as a way of helping me along. Perhaps he was also just a bit bored, having been turned away from The 21. It was always hard to tell.

Patsy looked doubtful.

'Well, I can't do anything,' he said, 'without first of all speaking to the old professor.' He meant Billy Hill – but Reggie didn't need to be told that. In fact, he really didn't need to be told any of that. It seemed to be an unnecessarily aggressive way of pointing out that Hill was more important than Reggie Kray. Patsy suddenly didn't look like quite such a friendly face.

'Can't ya?' said Reggie, his jaw clenched. He grabbed Patsy and between the three of us we dragged him into The Astor's office. We knew the manager and Reggie asked if he could use the telephone. It was polite enough but there was no mistaking the fact that Reggie was in charge now. He dug out Billy Hill's number and dialled as if it was a scheduled business appointment rather than just gone half past two in the morning. And Billy answered the phone as if he exchanged pleasantries with a Kray twin at that hour on a regular basis.

'Bill,' said Reggie, 'we've got a fella here who reckons he can't hardly talk to us, he can't do anything with us, without your permission.'

'Come over now,' said Billy. 'Bring him with you.' This was a suggestion that met with Reggie's approval, as wise old Billy Hill undoubtedly guessed. We kidnapped Patsy, bundling him into the car to take him to Hill's flat at 17 Moscow Road in Bayswater. It wasn't far but it was almost three in the morning as our mini gang arrived on Billy's doorstep. We were greeted by the man himself, relaxed in a Sulka designer dressing gown and cravat.

'Come in, Reg! Come in, boys!'

He was welcoming. A fully-stocked bar ran the entire length of one big room in his flat and the rooms were hung with immaculate flock wallpaper. He glowered at Patsy.

'Get in there, you!' he snapped. 'Get in the kitchen!' He served us all drinks and when Reggie was quite comfortable he listened sympathetically to his account of the evening's woes.

'Yeah?' said Billy at the appropriate moment. 'Patsy shouldn't have done that.'

'Well, we'll take him away with us,' said Reggie flatly. 'He's going in the drink tonight.'

This was his favourite way of saying he was going to kill someone. I don't know where he got it from. He probably just liked the sound of it.

'Oh, Reg,' said Billy quietly. 'Can't I just kick him up the arse and we'll throw him out?'

'Nah. It's very insulting, what he's done. I'm gonna do him. Throw him in the river.'

Billy tried a new tack.

'Look, out of respect for old times, don't. This is the last place he's been seen. And I ain't done anything. Please. Let me kick him out, can I?'

As if he was allowing a cheeky child an extra biscuit, Reggie said, 'Oh, go on, then!'

Billy thanked him and headed out to the kitchen. We just heard him begin to shout before the door closed and the sound was cut off. Billy was almost certainly saying, 'Quick, have it away, I've got you off the hook.'

When he came back, still resplendent in his dressing gown, he threw a little package into Reggie's lap. A chunky, sealed envelope.

'What's this?'

'There's a monkey there, Reg.' Five hundred quid. A lot of money at that time.

'No, Bill!' said Reg.

'Please! Would you please take it? I wanna give it to you. And if you take it and ever I need you, I'll feel that I can phone you up and speak to you. I just want to give you that as a token of goodwill, so we can be friends.'

Once again, as if he was doing a massive favour, Reggie nodded his agreement. I didn't get a penny out of it – which was typical of Reggie. One or two more gin and tonics for the road and we left, some of us quids in. Billy Hill himself had even more to celebrate. He told me himself – a long time afterwards, when the Krays had gone away – that he was grateful for Reggie's antics that night. The 21 Club had been straight on to Billy to say they'd had trouble with the Kray twins.

'Leave it to me,' he said.

He would handle it, he was the boss and they weren't to worry about it. And indeed, that's what he did. The 21 were indebted to him and now so was Reggie. The real result was all Billy's.

Billy Hill enjoyed the kind of reputation and respect that the twins could only dream about. And they did. He might not have the public image that the Krays had but nor did he want fame. He had made his life work in a way they never managed. When he celebrated his birthday at The Latin Quarter in Wardour Street, everyone of importance turned out. The doorman was Bert Hyland, a nice, old Irish ex-boxer. He not only organised car parking but arranged for vehicles to be returned home as far east as Upton Park while their owners toasted Billy – everything seemed to be more polished around him.

It was only a few days after Reggie had been at the flat that cunning Bill called in his favour. Reggie was to help him with some sort of problem but he didn't ask me because that would have meant sharing the cash. He asked me to stay by the phone at Vallance Road until he got back while he headed off with some likely looking characters from Aldgate. Whatever Billy wanted couldn't have been too serious judging by the way they all came back, laughing and joking.

'It was nothing,' Reggie told me. 'He was playing cards with some of his friends. They were just waiters from the local French restaurants. All he did was give us a few quid and say, "I was just trying you out. Sorry, Reg – I couldn't help it."'

They got a couple of grand for their trouble. But, as I discovered for myself much later, the scene had been far from an innocent wind-up. They had been completely taken in by Billy Hill. The 'waiters' were laughing at the Krays. And, more to the point, they weren't waiters.

When I was later more friendly with Billy, he explained it all to me.

'They were Unione Corse gangsters who ran all the gambling in the West End,' he said.

This was the French Mafia who operated out of places like Marseille and along that Riviera strip. Very powerful and worse than the Americans for cold-blooded killing. They had been into loads of casinos in London and they had made money from marked cards. It was through them that Billy had made most of his fortune – through crooked gambling at some of the top places in London.

He even had people in leading casino The Clermont in Berkley Square, Mayfair, and when they got found out he went to John Aspinall the owner to offer him a choice. Either watch the story leak and people lose confidence in him, or let them carry on and cut them in. So when all these people like Lord Lucan were gambling, it was all crooked. And they never knew. It was incredible, really. The French were so much more discreet than any of their English or American counterparts. There was none of that talk of 'taking over' that you heard in London. That Corsican heritage was evident in their secretive, patient approach to empire building. They were able to take over more than the likes of the Krays ever did.

To demonstrate his influence to his partners in the Unione Corse Billy sent for the twins and they dutifully came tearing in. He only wanted to show how he could raise a right mob at a moment's notice if he needed to. Reggie might have blustered to Billy but the truth was that both brothers were frightened of him. They knew that he was that much smarter than them even if they never knew how openly he used them to enlarge his own empire. Nobody ever found out how much Billy Hill manipulated them.

Patsy Murphy, the fella we met and Reggie went on to bully in The Astor, also wasn't who he seemed. Not just some aimless character who got about, he was instead a rick, one of Hill's own card players who worked with marked decks. There was some sort of contraption Billy got into casinos to mark the cards, he told me. Apparently the French used a wooden box which Billy said he improved on by making an aluminium version. I never got into the technical side because I wasn't ever into gambling. But however he did it, these devices would introduce a subtle bend to the cards which you could recognise if you had an eye for it and you would

132

be able to identify any card. The hardest part of Billy's scam was finding someone on the inside to ring the cards for marked decks. It would be a cleaner or waiter who could do that. Skilful ricks like Patsy joined the clubs and read the cards just as clearly as if they were seeing each one from the front.

Without realising it, Reggie had struck gold with Murphy when he piled in like a short-sighted, angry rhinoceros. Murphy was an important member of Billy's team who Billy moved quickly to defend, before with equal agility turning Reggie's blundering to his advantage. If only Reggie had half Bill's brains he might have worked out why the other man was so interested and gone on to use that for his own advantage. There was no chance of that. Reggie was just happy – as usual – to make a few quid.

And though I didn't know what was going on at the time, I had a feeling that they were being made fools of. There was something wrong there, even if it was hard to pinpoint exactly what it was. It was part of a wider sense of an ending. The Krays' little empire was on the decline. Their attention was diverted by the necessity of keeping an eye on other firms and families in London.

In the end, it would indirectly be their obsession with and failure to win against South London's Richardsons and their associates that would bring them down, though the catastrophe began with a brush with the Mafia.

Visiting Americans had opened up a casino in The Connolly Club in Berkeley Square. It was next door to The Astor and it was very glitzy. George Raft was the main man with the new arrivals. Everyone latched on to him and it was all good natured. The Americans were here to play, not to shoot anybody. I remember people like Joe Pyle were breaking their necks to be seen next to them when they went to fights and the twins visited them at The Connolly. There they made a bit of a nuisance of themselves.

A Jewish family were having a loud argument among themselves – father and son were getting a bit noisy. Ronnie jumped up and was all for going over to sort them out. George Raft calmed him down.

'Ron! They're customers! It'll be all right.'

Shortly afterwards George Raft pulled me aside and said, 'Has Ronnie met the Blade yet?'

The Blade being Charles Tourine, the top Mafia enforcer here. It was obvious to me that Raft thought that Ronnie could become a problem. He eventually came up with a good scheme for containing the Krays. He approached Reggie with a business plan.

'I can see things aren't going too well for you, if you don't mind me saying so.'

He meant financially. And he was right.

'I wanna offer you some money. I wanna do a deal. I'll give you £300 a week. You're the top firm here, the Nashes and you. And I'm going to give you £3,000 now as a down payment.'

You could interpret it as protection money, of a sort, though Raft had gone to Reggie voluntarily. He just wanted to avoid trouble.

And this was where the problems began. Ronnie immediately gave a third to Freddie Foreman and a third to the Nashes. The idea was to build some kind of coalition. He was very influenced by Winston Churchill's belief in the power of great alliances – he was a fan of Churchill in general and would often listen to recordings of his speeches.

'Great man, Churchill,' he would say. 'I will go to his funeral when he dies.' Unfortunately, he was in Brixton Prison when he died.

Reggie backed his idea. The Nashes were a formidable force and Freddie Foreman had his robbers to call on. It was the link to Foreman that would later prove to be toxic, though the twins hoped it would provide a defence against the Richardsons in South London. The Krays were afraid of their connection with Frankie Fraser. This was an ancient feud.

The young Krays had been friendly with Jack Spot while the South London lot, along with Bobby Warren, Billy Bly, Albert Dimes, Battles Rossi and co, had sided with Billy Hill when he ordered an attack on Spot. They then threatened the twins, who were at that stage too inexperienced to take them on. They never really got over it and were shocked when Fraser joined with the Richardsons on his release from prison. Frankie Fraser had a hex on them from then on and so did Billy Hill. The memory of that lingered. When Fraser came to a local pub to see the Krays, nobody touched him. He was more of a menace than the Richardsons themselves.

I knew how much the alliance meant to them, but I was still very disappointed that they had given all that money away. Ronnie's gesture might have been straight out of the statesman leadership handbook, but it meant that, once again, he had frittered away a useful source of income. By the time all three of the Krays had divided up the rest of the cash between them, there wasn't that much left.

Nobody else around the twins seemed to understand how important money was. Most of them just sat next to the twins all day like the family was some kind of labour exchange. There were a few exceptions like an old fella who was a friend of the Krays' father, known as The Plum because he had a blue face and a little fat neck. Ronnie rated him for going out and earning his own money, but mostly the Krays were surrounded by useless morons. Ronnie once addressed them all in a speech.

'I wanna speak to all you lot,' he said, specifically excluding me and a couple of other fellas who had a living. It was the rest of them who had got to him.

'I'm fucking fed up of you, you make me sick.' It was a bizarre, mad rant. 'I ain't asking you to be French gangsters! I ain't asking you to go out and cut people's throats! But why don't you go out and tap people like The Plum does, and he's 65? You're just sitting around skint all day.'

Maybe most of the mob around the Krays were on the dole and didn't need the money. Maybe they just didn't care.

As Ronnie's speech of frustration demonstrated, the twins knew they couldn't rely on their men for anything important, particularly the feud with their rivals. And this was more serious than the frequent, spontaneous fights which often came out of nowhere, though Freddie Foreman has claimed that the row with the Richardsons was no different. He was wrong. The twins were always plotting against them. Always. There was a big row in a Catford club called Mr Smith's between the Richardsons and Fraser and the Hennessey crew which was the main example. It has always been said since that this was an impulsive free-for-all, but that wasn't the case.

The Hennesseys asked Foreman, 'What happens if it's off? Are we all right to have a row?'

The message back from the twins was unambiguous – 'Definitely. We'll back you to the hilt.'

They did just that, arming the Hennesseys as well. The resulting battle has been extensively documented. The Richardsons had taken over security at the club, more as a kind of status thing than for the money. But what has always been denied was the involvement of the Krays – yet they were up for it. Within a couple of nights of asking permission, the Hennesseys staged an attack that seemed chaotic but was fully sanctioned by the twins.

Among the casualties was Frankie Fraser, shot in the leg, and Dickie Hart, who got killed. He went along with the Hennesseys and was thought of as a full member of the firm, though the twins never met him. The upshot of the row was that Fraser and Eddie Richardson got ten years each. I don't think any of the Hennessey mob got any bird. As a side note George Raft and his Mafia pals wanted no part of the row and caught the next plane back to the States. When they eventually tried to return to Britain the Home Secretary barred entry to them, probably saving the West End from falling under Mafia control in the process.

The twins were triumphant but they were too loud about it. I began to feel uneasy after meeting Reggie on my way to visit a couple of people at Dartmoor. I had been to the prison before and my routine was to try for a morning visit and that meant I would either be driven overnight or stay in a hotel. This time I dropped in at The Regency Club on my way to meet my driving partner. Reggie was outside the club. He grabbed hold of me, which was right out of character for such a buttoned-up fella, and pulled me on a wild waltz in the street.

'Ain't it great?' he said. 'What about that? It's wonderful!'

He was almost hysterical with joy at the result in Mr Smith's. I didn't like it. As I extricated myself from his embrace and walked off, I thought to myself, you shouldn't be doing this. You'll be next. This doesn't sound too good to me at all. It was all off, this gloating. There wasn't any need to be vindictive about it.

I was out of touch until my return to London the next day when I grabbed a couple of hours sleep. I bought the newspaper early that morning and near the back was the headline: MAN SHOT DEAD IN THE BLIND BEGGAR PUB. This was a total shock – the landlord was Patsy Quill who, along with his brother Jimmy, were friends of mine.

The shooting had to be bad news. I phoned Charlie, who told me to meet him that morning at Mile End Station. My question was only one word.

'Reggie?'

'No,' said Charlie. 'Ronnie.'

'What happened?'

'Mick,' he said quietly. 'It's a shame you wasn't around. Some nightclub hostesses from the West End spoke to Freddie Foreman.'

Freddie had The Prince of Wales in Lant Street near Borough Market. The girls told him that a Richardsons' firm member called Billy Stayton had got drunk and said he was going to throw a petrol bomb pub in Fred's pub. And while he could always have a fight, anyone with any sense knew that Billy wasn't ever going to carry out his pissed threats. But Freddie was close to the Krays, lived above the pub with his family, and so something had to be done.

'We'd have sent you over there, Mick,' continued Charlie, 'but who we sent over in the end was fucking Nobby Clark'

He was an ex-flyweight boxer, though he'd have been better off as a circus ringmaster. Extrovert, outgoing and theatrical, he was also a total nuisance. Loud voice, bald head. You couldn't fail to notice him and he was the last person you'd want to send on a delicate mission like this.

'It's all off!' he shouted on his return. 'It's off again. They're going to bomb Fred's pub!' And on he went. This set Ronnie off and with great relish he worked himself up into a state of battle readiness, every inch The Colonel about to lead his troops over the top. He grabbed two of his nearest men and ordered them to drive him to The Blind Beggar. And there can't be many people who don't know where the story is going.

'Who's in The Beggars?' said Charlie. 'George Cornell. Ronnie shot him, killed him stone dead. Oh God. We've won the war and now we're back in it. What are we gonna do?'

George Cornell, the Richardsons' man, shot in front of so many witnesses you'd think that Ronnie wanted to go down.

Poor Patsy Quill was driven fucking mad over the Cornell shooting. He and Georgie had known each other all their lives. Patsy was upstairs in The Blind Beggar when he heard two shots and came down to find Georgie slumped over.

The Old Bill took Cornell's body away and then said to Patsy, 'Scrape them up.' They pointed at Cornell's brains, blown all over the floor.

Shooting Cornell was the end for the Krays. It was as bad as it could be. They'd won a great victory over the Richardsons in Catford without having to fire a shot themselves. Charlie and I played it cool as we spoke but I could tell from looking at him that he knew it would be nearly impossible to pull things back. We were all stuck for our next move.

Eventually, Reggie suggested putting it about that it was nothing to do with the ongoing feud, but it was personal. Cornell had called Ronnie a poof. If we spread that story around, he hoped, maybe the Richardsons wouldn't try and retaliate. So that's what me and Charlie told Billy Hill.

Coincidentally, Billy Hill's favourite all-purpose insult was to say whoever was on the receiving end of his displeasure was 'a fucking poof'. He didn't react when we gave him the story. He just adjusted his cufflinks before looking back at us.

'What Ronnie does is his own business,' he said, dismissively. 'It doesn't concern anybody else.' I thought it was a magnificent response from Hillsy, and quite funny.

The legend of Ronnie's personal vendetta against Cornell was born. Billy had understood perfectly what we were doing and he didn't want anything to do with any of it. Years later, when we were good friends, he would say that's how he survived so long.

'I was the only one who could think,' he said, and I also found that any ability to reason put you ahead in the world of the twins.

There wasn't really any particular reason behind Cornell's death. It wasn't him calling Ronnie any names. It wasn't the feud. A lot of bollocks has been written about it since. Some have even claimed that George had once given Ronnie a right hiding. But I knew Cornell and he was friendly and amiable enough. Certainly not a particularly powerful geezer. He wouldn't have taken Ronnie on.

It was purely Billy Stayton and Nobby Clark's carry-on that led to the shooting and I can't emphasise how much damage they did. Before Nobby's performance the Krays had even been known to defend Cornell.

There was one time when Ginger Marks, who we all knew and who was also killed himself in a shooting, was in The Kentucky Club.

'Mick, I've just had a right touch,' he said. 'I want to ask you something. I'll give you a nice few quid if you do George Cornell for us.'

Marksy, also known as Tommy Marks, was known for being a bit impetuous. I had no intention of doing the job for him but didn't tell him outright. Meanwhile, I reported the encounter to Ronnie.

'What?' said Ronnie. 'Cornell's a friend of mine! He put me up when I was on the run!'

And so he went on, raging against Marksy's disrespect. He followed it up by frightening the life out of him. Cornell hadn't done anything to deserve his shooting. It could have been anyone in The Beggar that night. Poor old George.

Even Freddy Foreman thought the killing was unnecessary.

'You'd have thought he'd walk down the road from the pub a bit. Just wait for him to come out, if he was so determined to do it.'

The shooting was so self-destructive that you had to wonder if Ronnie wanted to bring things down. Perhaps that's looking too deeply into it. But while they would never have consciously wanted their lifestyle to come to an end, they knew they weren't going to go any further. Ronnie was certainly aware of it. Reggie, meanwhile, was just a shell of his former self.

Chapter Eleven

Leaving the Krays

Ronnie Kray was a shambling mess, drunken, pilled-up, telling any random stranger who would listen.

'I shot George Cornell, you know.' This was getting a bit boring. 'Did you like him?' he would mutter. 'Did you agree with it?'

The twins had been on the slide for a while but now everybody knew. From the moment of the killing in my friend's pub – and that was a fucking liberty without any point whatsoever – the insanity had gone public. I wanted out. But how could I get out? You couldn't just say a cheery 'Good day!' to the Krays.

Reggie was also beginning to cut a sad figure, skulking around, sticking to the streets in which he felt safest. The clubs were all going and the circle of Kray influence was shrinking to the two or three other pubs nearest their house. There they felt secure. When we were somewhere like The Grave Maurice there were loads of people. Partly that was because it was opposite London Hospital and, as my then friend Teddy Machin once observed, 'This place is full of surgeons.'

He looked at the medical staff up one end of the pub and the Krays at the other.

'Surgeons up there and surgeons down here.'

Yet as desperate as life was getting, Reggie could still hold a grudge.

'Mick! See that fella over there?' he said one night in The Maurice. 'I'm gonna chin him later. I'm going to stick it on him. Buller's just told me he's a grass.'

I kept my voice natural. 'No, he's not, Reg. I know him quite well. That's Bill Taylor.' AKA Bill the Blower, from Manchester. 'He's a nice guy. Good as gold. '

Bill was a very smart, good looking, veteran safe blower. But Reggie wouldn't be convinced now he'd heard it from Buller Ward – Buller the bully. A liar as well. He was the muscle who came to Paris with me.

'Old man Burns has told him,' said Reggie.

Burns was a waste paper merchant whose son was Tony Burns, a former amateur boxer who had taken over his father's boxing club, The Repton, in Bethnal Green.

'Look, Reg, leave it to me,' I said. 'I'll sort this out and if it's proven that Bill's a grass, I'll do him. That's how confident I am.' I went over to Bill and came straight to the point. It was the only way to deal with it. 'Do you know old man Burns?'

'Yeah, I know him quite well.'

'He's called you a grass.' Bill was clearly shocked. I filled him in with what Buller said. We decided to go and see Burns at his home ourselves just off Bethnal Green Road. He looked delighted to see us and Bill in particular.

Inside Bill asked him, 'Have you heard any stories about me being a wrong 'un? Anything like that?'

'Nah,' said Burns. 'Leave off, Bill. Everyone's got the utmost respect for you.'

'Buller's told the twins that I'm a grass!'

'Fucking liberty! My God, you're nothing of the kind.' It sounded sincere and that's what I told Reggie. I knew Buller was lying and that it was completely motiveless. Buller was just wicked. You get them. A nasty bastard.

The incident was put to one side for a while, but Buller was always on borrowed time. The one thing you really didn't want to be getting Reggie to do was to chin someone on your behalf – even now the twins were on the way out. Anything else might be forgotten but this would have niggled away at Reggie, no matter the state he was in.

Not long before they were nicked, by which time they were generally barely able to stand up most of the time, Reggie happened upon Buller and slashed him across the face. Even when Buller told others what happened, he couldn't help but embellish the story.

'He was walking past me and then turned and hit me on the chin. I said, "Is that the best you can do?"' said Buller.

There was no way that anybody would ask Reggie Kray a question like that. Buller never knew why he was attacked, but he had it coming.

Less welcome was the way that Reggie was starting to muscle in on my business. A friend called Kenny Johnson owned The Two Puddings in Stratford and he had asked me to do security.

'Can I give you a few quid every week? I'm not worried about local people coming in and causing trouble,' he said, 'the doorman can deal with all that. But if I have any bigger shots causing me problems, you could handle it for me or tell me what to do.'

That was how it worked. People were always nervous of the big names – if they'd heard of someone that was half the fight, at least until the name himself got done and then it started again. I was part of that system and not intimidated. For me it just meant regular money, if no fortunes.

Reggie became one of those problems. He had become obsessed with a load of one-armed bandits he had got into. Fruit machines.

But he just didn't know where to put them all. The upshot was he wanted to put a machine in my mate's pub. You might think that was a small request, but that was his foot in the door. He'd soon want what I was getting. I didn't give him an answer and trusted that he would forget about it. I knew how to handle him.

I had to do more to earn my money when Roy Shaw made himself a nuisance in the dancehall above the pub. He threw first his weight around and then Kenny down the stairs, just another day at the office for Roy Shaw but it frightened the life out of Kenny. He didn't know that I already knew Roy when he asked me for help. I got a message back to Roy through one of his associates.

'Tell your mate Roy Shaw that if he don't go in there and apologise, the next time I see him I'm going to shoot him.'

For a while nothing happened. I got back to the friend and asked him what the response had been. He claimed not to have seen Roy since we'd spoken, which I knew wasn't true but I didn't respond. I just waited until the night I saw Roy myself in The Two Puddings. He was at the bar with two friends, Denis Callaghan and Dicky O'Sullivan. I was with Johnny Davies. Roy was unmistakeable, as ever a proper old-style tearaway. When he was drunk and ready for trouble he stood against the bar, his hands spread awkwardly wide to hold himself up, snorting and jerking his head as he looked around the pub. Looking for a fight. He probably had a handful of purple hearts inside him as well. But he seemed to snap into focus when he saw me.

'Mick! How are you?' Roy said. 'Getting a few drinks in here. I've already apologised. What d'ya want to drink?' He was easy to deal with and the brooding trouble on the horizon faded away. Soon it was just the two of us after Johnny had to make an appointment at The Regency and Roy's friends went on to some other venue. Roy had an idea.

'Fancy going up the West End?' He'd just had a bankroll robbery at one of the national newspapers. 'I've got a load of notes that I'm just getting rid of. I'll take you out and it won't cost you nothing. We'll knock this money out.'

The cash was numbered and the police knew what had been taken. Somebody had to do some spending. Lovely! Right up my street!

The Bagatelle Club was in Cork Street in Mayfair and the owner took me aside when I was on my way to the toilet.

'I know you, don't I?' he said. 'Didn't you used to get down here before with Jacky Buggy and that lot?'

Jack was a Scottish fella who finished up in chains at the bottom of the sea. I did remember him and a couple of other names the owner mentioned from the same era. It was clear that he was just establishing common ground between us and he hurriedly got to the point.

'Look,' he said, 'see your mate? Is he all right?'

'Yeah, yeah. Good as gold.'

'Only he came down here the other night,' he whispered, 'and he was chewing the glasses.'

This was Roy's party trick – crunching pint glasses in his mouth and spitting out the debris without a cut to his mouth.

'Don't worry about it,' I said. 'He's all right when he's with me. Just don't stripe him up.'

I was suggesting that the owner didn't charge us too much. Me and Roy certainly hadn't held back – there was a good dinner, hostesses at the table and a vast amount of drink. But when the owner himself brought over the bill with a nervous smile it was for little more than a fiver. We were left with no choice but to spend more money elsewhere.

It was around 3.00 am when we headed off to an upstairs Soho speakeasy, though not one used by gangsters. It was more bohemian junky types and they weren't ready for Roy Shaw in full flow.

He charged behind the counter, pushing the barman out of the way and shouted, 'I'm gonna have a lay down! I'm tired!' There was a shelf under the bar and as Shaw tucked himself in he made a parting reference to me. 'And fucking look after him. 'Cos he's worse than me – he'll cut your throat!'

Roy also got mixed up with the Aldgate mob, another crew who were friendly with the twins, headed by Willy and Charlie Malone. They had quite a few people around them and Willy himself was a bookmaker with an SP office – SP for 'starting price', a racing term. He looked the part, though he was more fat than thick-set and he was smart and never short of money. They had a club in Brick Lane which I'd been to myself – more just a room with a bar than a proper venue. But it was somewhere to go at a time when the licensing laws made it impossible to go anywhere after 11.00 pm. Roy turned up – alone, drunk and boisterous, as usual. Willy asked him not to start trouble and that immediately got Roy going.

'I'm just being friendly, I only want a drink. I don't want no trouble. Look!' He pulled out a huge knife. 'If I was looking for trouble, I wouldn't show you that, would I? I don't even want it.' He threw the knife to one side and Willy – who could handle himself – chinned him. The drunken Shaw was out with the one punch.

Willy didn't know Roy Shaw, but everyone was quick to tell him that it wasn't any old drunk he'd dealt with. Although Roy was aware that Willy knew the twins, Roy wouldn't care, they said. He'd be back. Feeling cornered, Willy took the first opportunity to head over to the twins, who did nothing.

Late one night Willy was out in his area with one of his firm.

'Me and you better take a walk,' said Roy Shaw, who had appeared alongside him. Willy said nothing but, mesmerised, followed Shaw around the corner where he was beaten up. After that he stayed firmly at the side of the twins, a cap and plaster hiding his wounds. It was a shock to his system. Willy wasn't as fierce as people thought he was. Anyone could be good at dishing it out – it was when it was coming back that the line was drawn.

The twins got hold of me. Would I do Shawry for them? They wanted him dead and they didn't know or care how well I knew him. I agreed with conviction, though I had no intention of doing it. It was a while before I ran into Roy again, by chance, at a popular tailor called Woods in Kingsland Road. Roy looked shocked. He'd heard that the twins were unhappy.

'God, I'm glad it's you,' he said. 'I thought it was the other two! I was just going to jump right through that window.'

The Krays' whims were becoming ever more bloodthirsty and less rational by the day. At a meeting in our new venue, a bungalow in Walthamstow, we discussed having Billy Stayton killed for his part in getting George Cornell shot. The twins and Freddie came along to hear that a friend of his had agreed to ready-eye him. This meant getting the trust of the victim so you could position them somewhere they could be targeted. All of this for someone who had just been a bit mouthy. I didn't believe it was really going to happen and I didn't want any part of it. They asked me anyway.

'Will you shoot Stayton?'

'Yeah,' I said flatly.

I thought, Here we go again. It was just like the business with Roy Shaw in some ways, but I was no longer certain they would just forget it if I just did nothing. They seemed to be increasingly obsessed with killing anyone they had a problem with. Their lust for blood was unrestrained now they knew that Cornell's killing had left them so publically exposed. In a sense, there was no option but to keep going.

They knew Cornell was the end. Reggie certainly did. By that time Frances was in a bad way, his drinking was out of control and his nerves were playing him up. He couldn't do it. He could not live that life any more. Nobody knew quite how bad it was but then came the night we were going out somewhere, walking from the house in Vallance Road and in the dark I saw him pop something in his mouth.

'What's that, Reg?' I asked. He told me it was Librium – prescribed for anxiety – and he was taking loads of it.

'I get this buzzing in my head,' he explained, 'and this stops it.'

His personality disorder was becoming much worse. He never had the outright mental illness that his brother suffered from and he would never be admitted into a secure hospital like Ronnie, but he was losing it. Their health wasn't helped by the imposters like Joe Pyle from Wimbledon, among many others from all over London. They were all over them. The madder they got, the more the newcomers liked it. It was like meeting the celebrities; the Krays' press was telling them they were invincible.

At the meeting I agreed to every detail for the killing of Billy Stayton. Freddie Foreman said he would put a car in a certain location. The boot was to hold a sawn-off shotgun. Billy was to be driven to a pub on Hackney Marshes and we would be assisted by Albert Donaghue, a fella who some have said was given an initiation by the twins. You can read elsewhere that they shot him in the leg to see if he'd go to the police and when he didn't he was accepted. Whoever wrote that needs to be shot in their own leg. It's complete rubbish. He was shot for sticking up for Lenny Hamilton and just another reason why I find it so hard to read some of those books.

We left the meet and I got into Freddie's Citroen. He showed me how the suspension could be moved up and down to compensate for weight.

'Fred,' I said once we pulled off, 'don't bother to put that gun in the boot. In fact, don't bother with the car because I'm going. I'm finished. I don't want to know. I'm off the firm.'

'Hmm,' was all he said.

I said, 'I don't want to know. All them fucking people they've got round them, I don't know them, I don't know their backgrounds. They'll be putting it on them all eventually. This is ridiculous! Leave me out of it. I won't be turning up. Drop me off.'

I got out in Cable Street and I went home and I forgot about them.

The next time I had anything to do with the Krays would be when we all shared a cell together. Except for the one move that Reggie made. He looked for me at The Two Puddings, but not alone – he couldn't do anything alone. A mug – an ordinary person – might not know who he was and try it on with him. It was a bit awkward so he always had to have a few people around him. One defeat and he'd be finished. Tommy Brown, big and impressive, a monster of a man, was typical of the accompanying muscle. But on this occasion Reggie took a gamble and came with his wife, Frances.

Reggie asked about me in the pub in a very friendly way. I knew how friendly Reggie was. If I'd have been there he would have invited me back and I would have taken the place of Jack the Hat. Jack McVitie – he was famously the friend and associate of the Krays killed for stepping out of line and making a nuisance of himself. It would be one of the crimes which would be used to put the twins away for good and it might well have been that I could have been an addition to the charge sheet. Reggie might not even plan to kill me there and then, but his mood would have changed.

At least Ronnie was more up front. I heard his view on my leaving from Bertie – my friend who'd been involved in some of the fighting with the Readings, who worked in The Regency, where everyone now tended to gather late at night. Bertie was a popular bloke and everyone liked him. He reported that Big Pat had said – and I knew it would have sounded even more preposterous in Pat's broad Scottish accent – 'Ronnie's got the fucking needle with Mick, you know. He's bought a machine gun and he's gonna fucking shoot him.'

It wasn't actually that dangerous to walk away as I did. Not because the twins wouldn't want to get me. Of course they would. I wasn't alone in leaving – two or three others, including Ronnie's loyal helper Johnny Davies, came with me or shortly afterwards. But the twins just didn't know how to take us out. They were simply not able to find their way around town on their own. The fellas who surrounded them at the end didn't know me. The Lambrianou brothers' biggest crime was robbing a Wimpy Bar. One of them said that in a book. That was their level. They weren't going to help.

The twins were too out of it to do much by then, but at the best of times they just weren't capable of searching properly and it was very unlikely they would see the value in coming after us as they knew we wouldn't just roll over and they could get done themselves. It wasn't out of benevolence, but rather incompetence. They'd lost it. And yet I wasn't stupid. I knew that while they were at large there was always a danger, however small. I was told by one of my mates that the last thing governments do before they go to war is to withdraw diplomatic relations. I thought about talking, but decided against it. The only way out was to get out and stay out and either wait for their empire to unravel, or get them ourselves.

I was still too cautious to get too cocky. At times I would think, hmm, yes, I'm skating on thin ice here. To rely on luck for them to fall apart before they stumbled upon us would have left us exposed.

Instead we watched the Krays' firm and waited for an opportunity to shoot first. My plan was not necessarily to kill the brothers. Even if you just winged one or other twin, that would be enough. They were always armed now and the police would have got them for a start. And their reputation for being untouchable would be ruined. The mighty Krays couldn't walk around in public with an arm in a sling. That would be enough to break the spell. They were mad as March hares by now and they wouldn't hesitate to do it to us. That's why we started to hear stories like the one about the machine gun, though that was never seriously more than one of Ronnie's fantasies. He'd have had his fingers off trying to assemble it.

Reggie had no such problems when he went after Nobby Clark himself. Nobby later told me about it in Bow Street Court.

'He came to me house and he put one in me scotch.' Nobby meant leg and he had no idea why Reggie shot him. As far as he could work out, he'd said something out of order about Frances. Nobby never did find out that he was targeted for being the one whose outburst had led directly to Cornell's murder.

Reggie must have known the real culprit for Cornell's killing was his twin brother. Yes, Nobby had been inexcusably stupid, but Ronnie pulled the trigger. Ronnie was to blame but how could his faithful Reggie ever admit that? He couldn't say, 'I wish this hadn't happened.' It just wasn't in him to say that about anything Ronnie did. The frustration built and Nobby was a stand-in for the feelings he couldn't allow himself to express. The closest he could get was when he met Jimmy Quill in another pub not long after the killing.

'What could I do, Jim? What could I do?' was all he said.

I might not have been at the same sort of risk as Billy Stayton but the Krays were increasingly erratic and that was dangerous for everyone. Reggie even fought with his own brother, Charlie. They were outside The Carpenters pub and under covert surveillance by those of us who'd left them, with the exception of Johnny Davies who, while handy to have around as loyal muscle, was too much of a moron to be any help.

We couldn't leave it to chance that the Krays would never find us. Another night I was with a mate in a car outside The Carpenters, a pub owned by the twins near Brick Lane.

Reggie happened to come out and my friend said, 'I'll shoot him now. I'll get out of the car and shoot him now.'

'No. In your own car?' I said. 'Leave off.'

It wasn't necessary for anyone else to take the risk. I'm not trying to make out that I could take them all on myself – quite the reverse, in fact. Freddie Foreman's lot would have been a major risk if they could have been bothered to come after us. But his men were sick of it all by now, they realised that they weren't getting anything out of the alliance. What they knew was robbing banks – big time. It might have been hard work but the easy money promised by Fred and the twins was turning out to be a mirage.

If Freddie wasn't a threat, I knew none of the idiots around the twins were going to come near those of us who left because they knew we were well armed. They all remembered the night in The Hammer Club when Johnny Davies shot Russy Bennett in the bollocks. If the Krays were going to get us there would be no use going after one or two – they'd have to make sure they took us all out.

Chapter Twelve

Assassinate Reggie

The phone rang. It was the code that said the way was clear to get Reggie.

'Your girl's been down here'. This was Bertie at The Regency. He had been observing the twins at the club. 'She's leaving with a geezer,' he continued, 'about now. He lives at Albert Bigg Point in Stratford.'

The plan was underway. We were going to make the first move against the Krays tonight.

Bertie was a good person to have within the firm. He was quite tough for a little bloke but he wouldn't start trouble. All he cared about was jazz. He was a music fanatic and very reliable. In our code, Reggie was 'my girlfriend' and that way he could say what was going on at The Regency while using the club's phone.

I got driven to the block by a fella I'm not going to name and we waited. I hadn't ever killed anyone before – and in the end I never did, though there would be times when I was only lucky not to have finished someone off. But I was ready to do it. We felt cornered by having left the Krays.

We had decided to make an exhibition of Reggie. We would shoot him, cut his throat and leave him outside the lift. Nobody would know who was behind it and the message would be far more effective that way. Reggie was expendable and it wouldn't have been doing humanity a disservice, would it? Maybe it would solve all my financial problems, I was thinking. Perhaps I could pick up where they left off.

He never turned up that evening but we weren't bothered. I was pretty sure the twins hadn't got any warning and we were determined to keep going until we got them, although, as it turned out, there wasn't going to be time to set up another attempt. It was just as well.

Killing one or both of the twins wouldn't have solved anything. It wasn't my smartest plan and it was one for which I would inevitably have been nicked for. Perhaps I even knew that at the time. But sometimes there is just nowhere else to go. The pressure under which I operated around the Krays had been intense. It always had been. At any point they might have discovered one of my freelance long firms or just taken against something I said. They might not have been that agile or as together as their legends have made out, but if I got in their way I would have been trampled before I even knew they were coming for me. Now it was so much worse. I no longer even recognised the world they lived in.

I had once known everyone around the Krays but now they killed time with a largely new crowd. Many would later claim to be good and long-time friends. And at the same time, increasing numbers of celebrities were attracted to their name. The underworld was open for public inspection. At least the twins wouldn't have to worry about being alone as they raced towards oblivion.

Everyone knew what was going on. And I mean everyone.

When I went all the way down to Dartmoor on another visit to a friend, he said, 'You know Mitchell's…?' he crossed his hands over his chest like a corpse laid out. This was Frank Mitchell, an associate of the Krays, and even I didn't know that he had been killed, the latest disaster for the twins. And here I was learning London secrets in the middle of Dartmoor Prison!

Mitchell – the press called him the 'mad axeman' – had escaped with the twins' help from a working party outside the prison. He had been a friend of the Krays and it was said they were mounting a campaign to get him the release date that the authorities just wouldn't give him. Terrible – just not to know when your sentence would end. But like anything the Krays did that required even basic planning, their real motivation was publicity. It wasn't out of loyalty.

You could imagine Reggie getting very excited, thinking about taking Mitchell down The Astor. Great big Frank Mitchell, known throughout the prison system. Everybody was terrified of him. He had the run of Dartmoor. When they went out on a work party they left him in the pub and the screw let him know what time he was to be picked up. Anything for a peaceful life with Frank – he was like long-time prisoner Charlie Bronson is today, except Mitchell was twice the size and one of the strongest men in the world. He was nice enough, though. Friendly – but a half-wit. A bicycle thief, albeit one with massive muscles and incredible fitness.

The twins didn't even need to break him out. All they had to do was to send Albert Barry in a car to the pub to pick him up – rather less impressive than organising the great escape from Dartmoor. But the follow-up was much less successful. A fella named Teddy Smith was engaged to write a letter – probably because he was the only half-literate one among the Krays, to the effect that Mitchell would give himself up in return for a date.

The Home Office was run by Roy Jenkins MP at the time and as Home Secretary he later caused the underworld no end of trouble by telling the police to concentrate on criminals rather than solving individual crimes, as a result of which they started to do their research properly. Under Jenkins the Home Office stopped Mitchell as well, placing a note in the paper to the effect that they would agree to a date if he gave himself up – and said where he'd been since his escape.

The twins were cornered and Mitchell himself was getting antsy.

'I can't stand it,' he said. 'I give up one prison for another! I don't like it here. This is driving me mad.'

Reggie consulted Billy Hill and Hillsy himself later told me what they'd done. He had nothing but contempt for the Krays and wasn't shy in the way he expressed it.

'Those brainless cunts!' he called them.

He stayed well out of it after having offered a few thoughts on the original letter, which he noted with scorn they couldn't put together on their own. I later found out it was Freddy Foreman who killed Frank Mitchell.

The worrying aspect of the death for the Krays was the way I heard about it – on that visit to Dartmoor. They all knew what had happened even if the details weren't yet out.

'It's all over here,' my friend said. 'Everybody fucking knows.' And that wasn't the only sign of the breakdown of secrecy.

Bertie asked me over to his place in Canning Town.

'There's a funny old turn-out,' he said. 'I think there's a bit of a sad story gone on. I think they've done Jackie McVitie last night.' More news spreading faster than was wise. 'Give me until tomorrow,' he continued, 'and I'll tell you exactly what's happened. Jack might have gone away again or something, I don't know. He was pissed and saying, "The twins don't fucking frighten me, I'm not frightened of anybody," and all things like that. Paralytic drunk. Pilled up as well.'

I already knew I'd done the right thing in leaving them but I could tell that this was a major development. As soon as he was about the next day, at tea-time, I went back to Bertie's.

'A sorry tale,' said Bertie. 'They lured Jack to a party in Evering Road,' and he gave me all the details of what would later be the well-documented killing of Jack the Hat.

It was still quite some time after then that the police got to hear about the killings but I wasn't at all surprised when the twins were nicked. The Evering Road party was full of people. They sent the women over the road but there were too many people watching. It was only a matter of time before the police caught up over those two deaths and Cornell.

I heard about their arrest from a friend in a phone call.

'The others have been nicked.' I thought, oh, right. Well, that will do. This was not long after I'd sat in the car waiting to shoot Reggie myself. My mates and me had been prepared to take them all on because we knew that some day we would end up having a battle with them. An arrest was the only other way it could have gone.

I had an errand to run to my parents' house and Bertie from The Regency happened to be with me. My mother looked panicked as she opened the door.

'Go away, go away,' she whispered. 'The police have been round. They're looking for you!'

Neither she nor my father knew what I was up to. They were straight but she knew I was in trouble and she was worried for me. I don't like to dwell on what I put them through – it would give me nightmares. They must have been so anxious as me and Bert jumped back in the motor.

I had thought that I had been out of it long enough for it not to concern me. I knew from having kept the twins under close surveillance that the police could have nothing on me relating to the murders. This had to be to do with something else. We drove past my house and I saw an unmarked police car, given away by its communications aerial. I got dropped off, knowing I would be better off alone. The anonymity of a bus would be much better for transport and I couldn't stay in my own home.

I moved into a hotel called The White House in Regent's Park. It was there that my brother phoned to say that our dad had lung cancer. There was no warning and he was only in his early 60s. He had gone into hospital feeling some pain and they operated to find the cancer. But I couldn't leave the hotel. My distractions were television and the newspapers and if nothing else there didn't seem to be anything for me to worry about, no case for me to worry about. Eventually, I thought it would be safe to return home to Plaistow. My white Rover was waiting for me in the garage and I returned to my life as usual. I had indeed got away with it – almost.

A month later the police swooped mob-handed and arrested me.

'A bit of luck catching you,' one said, 'as nobody put it on you.'

I had nothing to do with the murders and the police had missed the long firms, though they had taken some interest in the Krays' business dealings. Instead it was down to the less discreet of my two sisters, who lived four doors away from the McVities, that I got into trouble. She was on nodding terms with Jack's wife and was fascinated by their world. She would name-drop that her brother – me – knew all these people and she loved finding out who knew what. She also bought Jack McVitie's old van. That was when the Fawcett name came up. The Old Bill had taken their time to get the investigation right. They put themselves all over the East End, being very friendly to everybody in order to get a good reputation with the people they wanted to trust them enough to give evidence.

'We're thinking Jack may be in his van at the bottom of the river somewhere,' said one Old Bill. 'What we wanted to do was eliminate it and we come across you. So that was handy, wasn't it?'

I didn't exactly agree but I didn't have much choice now but to get in their car.

We drove to West End Central Police Station where I was grilled about my involvement with the Krays. The interviewer indicated a stack of papers and said, 'That is about you.' They made a great deal out of my having run Esmeralda's, but that was a sign of desperation. I never left many clues and they didn't have anything on me.

The Krays' former financial adviser, Leslie Payne, and his friend had left them and later put it on the twins. They were terrible. They also provided evidence against me, although I'd never dealt with either of them. Payne said I'd been involved in some dodgy company, which I hadn't been. It didn't really matter to the police. The point of the exercise was to get the Krays and Foreman and to find something to get anyone who had been involved in any way assisting them. At the end of what turned out to be an extremely long day, I was charged only with conspiracy in connection with the long firms and they had to give me bail.

What should have been a routine committal hearing at Bow Street Magistrates' Court was a sensation with the Krays at the heart of it. Television cameras were there every day, following the vans as they went to and from the prison. The Old Bill all had guns. I loved the excitement and prepared myself by doing my best to look as unlike a Kray as possible. I had on a green tweed three-piece suit and bought a copy of *The Financial Times* because it was pink. With *The FT* rammed smartly under my arm I was escorted to a cell containing all those people I'd not spoken to for a long time. All of the Kray team were being tried together. There were 13 of us in there in total. It was strangely quiet in there and I stood away from them at one end of the sizeable cell. The contrast was marked. They were all in the trademark East End gangster outfit while I stood out and away from them in every possible sense.

I knew I was at risk from reprisals but I was also aware that the authorities were not going to give me a choice of accommodation. What could I do? I stood with my back to the wall and looked as non-aggressive as possible. The twins must have thought I would turn but the reality for me was I knew there were others in that cell who would end up giving evidence. I didn't have any incentive. The police had nothing on me and I wasn't going to run the risk of incriminating myself for no reason, was I? But I knew the twins couldn't be sure of that and I expected a confrontation at any moment. There would have been 12 witnesses, but when had that ever stopped Ronnie before? The expected assault never came. It was baffling.

They certainly weren't frightened of me in a physical sense. If nothing else they could easily have overpowered me but perhaps they just didn't know who they could trust around them. Or maybe it was the policeman who brought them down, 'Nipper' Read, who inadvertently helped me out. He searched me in the cell on the second day and that must have provided a hint that I wasn't about to give evidence.

Even so, this was the Krays' last chance to take revenge on me for having walked away, but they failed to take it. I don't think they really knew what to do with me. I was a bit of a strange case, having left them without a word and seemingly without motivation, and here we were all in rather unusual circumstances, eyeballing one another directly under the court in Bow Street. What conversation there was tended to be between the three Krays and Limehouse Willy.

For two weeks we were based in that one cell during the procedures, filing out for our appearances every day and all that time the only person to approach me at all was big Tommy Brown, the gruff gypsy.

'Why are you blanking me, son?' he growled. 'I ain't done fuck all to you.'

'No, but plenty of you want to,' I said. He grunted and walked away.

Whenever we were in the dock, I left a space between me and the rest of them. I craftily meant to suggest that I didn't like them and I wasn't going to have anything to do with them. If there was any influence I could exert on the magistrates it would be that I was separate from the Kray firm. However you wanted to put it, my attitude said, I was a different race, another breed. Whatever might keep me from their fate. It worked.

On the last day after lunch the jailers asked, 'Do you mind if we move you up a row, much nearer the twins?' I said I didn't.

Despite all my careful attempts to distance myself, I was actually a bit mad myself at the time, a very confident character.

It will sound completely bizarre to say it but I have to admit I was enjoying being in the courtroom. The officer looked relieved.

'A few of the others have made statements against the Krays,' he said, 'and they're frightened that when the balloon goes up it will be on them all.' Among those who turned was none other than trusted associate Limehouse Willy, the very one they'd been chatting to so much in the cell.

The trial at the Old Bailey that would follow the committal has been well documented, with Ronnie insulting the prosecutor at every opportunity. But the twins also put on a little double act while they were at Bow Street, which was not so well reported. Reggie got himself on his feet on the second day.

'Can I speak? Can I speak?' He wasn't usually a natural public speaker, tending to mutter. 'I want to make a complaint. Mr Read and his men have taken my granddad's pension book away.'

The magistrate looked irritated. 'I'll make a note of that,' he said, 'for what it's worth.'

Ronnie, still sitting, looked with open disgust at the magistrate. '"Make a note of it"? You old cunt!'

Like his brothers he knew it was all over. In that sense there was little point in trying to make things better for himself and he could barely follow the case half the time anyway. He'd clearly resolved to have fun while he still could. The magistrate decided the best course of action was to talk through this and he did what he could while Ronnie continued to repeat 'old cunt' to the delight of the other defendants. Even the police couldn't keep their faces straight.

As the last one to be nicked, I was the last to take my seat in the dock. Walking up the stairs my eyes happened to lock with Freddie Foreman. He didn't flicker, just looked down. Since the day I left the car after we discussed killing Stayton, we've never exchanged a word.

Albert Donoghue, who was also in on the plan to kill Stayton, turned and put it on Foreman. I've still got the transcript of the committal proceedings with my own very brief statement.

'I've got nothing to say about the Kray twins.'

The atmosphere in the courtroom altered after that. Now at last the others knew what I was up to – nothing.

Bobby Buckley, Ronnie's boyfriend, later said to me, 'We all thought you'd grassed when you blanked us all, Mickey.'

The committal continued with an old mate of mine – and former good friend to the twins – giving evidence for the prosecution. Billy Exley was recovering from a heart attack and spoke from a wheelchair.

When it came to the charges against me he said, 'Fawcett said to me, "I think this is crooked, Bill, I'm going," and he wouldn't have anything to do with it.' That was enough to get me off.

My solicitor stood up to defend me but the magistrate waved him into silence.

'I don't think you need to speak,' he said. 'There are clearly major flaws in the evidence against Fawcett. He's discharged.'

I stood up immediately and made to leave. And Charlie Kray shouted out with great warmth but poor timing, 'Oh, good luck, Mick! Well done!'

Two of us were freed, me and Sam Lederman.

Charlie was to suffer again as a result of his family name. He made a lot of contacts up north and in the Midlands after his release, living with a girl in Leicester, but he wasn't intelligent enough to know how to deal with so many admirers. He had a sort of Krays' supporters' club and it was one of them who finished him off some years later.

In 1996, Charlie had gone to the funeral of his son Gary, who had died of an HIV-related illness. A member of his new group of friends came to the funeral with a driver who, as Charlie went on to write in his own book, introduced him to what turned out to be undercover police. He set them up with a cocaine supplier and they nicked him. You could say it was the Krays' celebrity status as much as anything that destroyed them all in the end. Charlie got 12 years and died in prison. Ronnie was also never freed before his death in 1995 and Reggie was allowed out a few weeks before he died in 2000, the same year as Charlie.

I still miss Reggie. I can go a long time without thinking about him and I can even be glad he's gone and that we didn't speak for so long. But then I'll think of some incident – and it might be one of his madder, more violent moments – and think, yeah, he showed them there for a while. Like the night we went for a drink in The Senate Rooms Club.

It was an unremarkable evening, quite dull, in fact, until we visited the toilet. I was just mid-slash when I was deafened by a tremendous explosion that made me think I might have permanent hearing damage. The noise of a gun going off in a bright, echoing space like a toilet makes you forget what's going on. I couldn't work out for a moment what had happened until I saw Reggie put the gun away in his pocket. The bloke standing next to us at the urinals had dropped to the floor, bleeding from the leg. His name, I found out later, was Ginger Cooper. Never saw him before, never saw him again and I didn't know what he'd done to receive such punishment, but he came from Hoxton and that would have probably been a good enough reason in Reggie's mind. Reggie and I strode calmly out of the toilets, through the club and into the night. Nobody tried to stop us, in fact, I stopped and had a chat with Terry Gill the boxer on the way out but I could tell Reggie was worried about something.

'I think I shot him in the head,' he said.

'No, it was definitely the leg,' I said.

'No, but as I shot him the gun jumped and he put his hands up to his head,' said Reggie.

'That was because it was so loud,' I said.

There was no further comment or explanation from Reggie. When I mentioned it to another friend of ours they seemed to know who the man was.

'Oh, what's he want to shoot Soppy Cooper for?' That was as much as I ever found out.

The next day Reggie seemed keen to talk about the night – but only in as much as he wanted to tell me about a terrible nightmare he'd had in which I was running over rooftops in the dark. The shooting was never mentioned again.

Chapter Thirteen

The Steamship

Billy Hill invited me out to join him at his apartment in Spain. After all the chaos with the last days of the Krays it was a completely different experience to spend time with someone who was so successful. I was even more interested when he offered to get me into the gambling games which had made him so much money.

I met Billy through a mutual friend, Teddy Machin, who was himself the most gangster-type gangster I'd ever seen in my life. He was about 6ft 1, he had black hair and he had black eyes. He knew how to dress and he had the walk. You'd think he was Sicilian. They used to call him Terrible Ted and he was the king of the Upton Park mob. He would end up being a bit of an uncle figure to my son, until we fell out. Teddy had been doing some driving for me while I was working on a long firm and I told him about the time that Reggie kidnapped Patsy Murphy and went to visit Billy and his 'waiters'. This tale duly made its way back to Hillsy who was intrigued to meet me.

He had a nice flat near Torremolinos in Spain and was as friendly and welcoming as I remembered him. We chatted about various people and places we'd known and Billy took me on a tour of the Costa del Sol, which back then was very pretty and not at all developed. We went to the Marbella club before returning to his place. Hillsy was never without 200 Benson & Hedges and smoked like a chimney. Taking out a cigarette, he rolled it between his hands until the tobacco dropped out. Perhaps he was going to replace it with marijuana. I'd been offered that before, but it didn't do anything for me. That one occasion was the end of drugs for me as far as I was concerned. I wasn't interested. But what Billy had was something different – he called it kief, a Moroccan cannabis derivative and this was good stuff. I've never come across it since. Having rolled it up, he presented it to me along with a stunning young French woman called Lilianne Satine. She used to sunbathe on the roof above Billy's place and she was tanned and golden, with elegant gold sandals. Having made the introduction, Billy fucked off with Machin and left me there with his drugs and the beautiful young woman. I realised that this was just his way of putting me at ease. Hillsy didn't drink, though he was utterly obsessed by women and liked his drugs a lot too – I guess that this was just his version of a gin and tonic.

The next day we were lounging around the pool and I said, 'A pal of mine named Boy Boy Clifford has bought a piece of land out here near Madrid. He's going to open a shooting club.'

'Do you realise that what you've just said could make you a fortune?' said Billy. 'Shooting clubs are about the only place in Spain where you can legally gamble. Now, I tell you, I have got friends in the Unione Corse. I'll put you in it. I'll introduce you to the main man. We'll do it up in Madrid.'

This contact was Marcel Francisci – the Unione Corse boss himself. Billy was obsessed with playing cards and understood *chemin de fer* backwards. If ever he had time to kill with someone, out would come the deck. Our conversation drifted to the twins and Billy once again called them 'those brainless cunts'. That was when he told me what had really gone on when Reggie got involved with Billy and the French 'waiters' and how they had in reality been Unione Corse.

Billy's own brother-in-law, Mickey Riley, was a talented rick. In Billy's own colourful phrase, 'a right berk with money, but he can read the cards. I'll introduce you to him too. He can graft with you. I gave him £100,000 last year and he ain't got a fucking penny now.'

I did meet him and he was indeed a right berk with money. Though he might fool you after Billy let him loose in the clubs. He wasn't very bright but you didn't need to be as long as you could read the cards.

Billy himself was very impressive – certainly in comparison to the likes of Riley, but also in contrast to the Krays. He had once hired a yacht in South Africa with a full crew. One of his right-hand men was Georgie Walker – one-time owner of the Trocadero in Piccadilly Circus. A very wealthy guy. After the Krays I got to know Billy's circle well.

In turn I later introduced him to a friend of mine called Jimmy, a good-looking geezer – though not a villain. Jimmy was very likable. Everyone seemed to get on with him and Hillsy was among them. Jimmy ended up doing odd jobs for Billy, sometimes walking his dogs. They were equally sex mad and Billy even made a play for his wife in front of him. Jimmy had only just introduced Maureen when Billy said, 'If ever you've got time and you fancy it, give me a ring. He won't know.'

Billy's own partner was Phyllis, though she was always called Gyp – a shortening of Gypsy. Billy was proud of her.

'She had a geezer's eye out with a glass, you know,' he would tell me. 'Everyone's frightened of her.'

Billy himself would get violent on drink and he made a point of never having anything to do with it. Gyp knew that and when he got up and left his birthday party to go to the toilet, she suggested that someone put 'a large of gin in his orange juice. That'll liven the old bastard up.'

Billy and Gyp had separate rooms in the Bayswater flat. 'I can have any birds up here I want,' he said, 'as long as I don't take them in her bedroom.' She was part of the swindle, as we used to say – when they first met she had been a brass.

Hillsy would also advertise in the Bayswater area for help in his flat and when girls rang up he would say something to let them know exactly what he wanted. That was heaven for Jimmy and it gave him further encouragement to do work for Billy just so he could spend time around him. Taking acid was another way that Billy found of heightening his sexual adventures. I have no idea what he got out of it but he had it all worked out. To counter the effects of the trip he would take one of his stash of incredibly strong sleeping pills to knock himself out. Jimmy thought this was hilarious.

But there was a darker side to Hillsy that never reached the public, though Jimmy got to see it. He interrupted a terrible scene at Hillsy's one day when he arrived to see a woman of mixed race with scars up her back, he later told me, as if she'd been slashed by a razor at some point in her life. This woman was setting about Hillsy, punching him and Billy yelled for help. They got her to the floor and Billy tied her hands with tape before they managed to get her into another room and lock the door. Jimmy was still shocked when he told me the whole story.

'A right fucking turnout,' he said. 'After a while she must have gone to sleep or something and I left.' He hadn't wanted to find out what had been going on and neither did I. But that wasn't the end of it. When he was next at the flat, Billy took him to one side.

'Don't ask no questions. She's dead and buried,' said Billy flatly. 'I couldn't put up with that sort of behaviour, could I, Jim?'

And the woman was never mentioned again. I can't say I was entirely surprised to hear what had happened. It reminded me how Billy would sometimes tell me about poisoning people. I hadn't paid him much attention at the time. But I also knew from Jimmy that Billy had put methadrine in ice cubes he served in drinks to girls in his flat.

I thought about the woman again many years later. A Justin Hill started being mentioned on the internet not so long ago. He was brought up by Gyp and he said his father was Billy Hill. Yet he was mixed race. The story was that Billy had spent a lot of money adopting him from a children's home where he was being ill-treated. But there was no word on his real mother and it seemed to me as if she could well have been the woman that Jimmy saw that day.

Other disturbing stories about Billy began to come out. Mikey Harris, a fella from over the Elephant & Castle, was older and had known Billy from way back.

'There's something wrong with that man,' Mikey said. 'He hates animals and he hates children. He's got to have something wrong with him.'

He had been slashed by Billy after a joke that went wrong. It was Billy's birthday and Mikey gave him a can of corned beef – it was a reference to an argument that Billy had with someone else over a stolen lorry load of the stuff. Mikey was always a comedian, but Billy didn't see the funny side.

As for the animal hatred, it was also true that Billy kept two standard poodles. But for Teddy Machin this in itself was suspicious.

'There's something funny going on with them two dogs,' he said. 'He gives them choice cuts of meat. He wouldn't fucking do that for no reason. There's something *funny* going on with those dogs.' Knowing Billy's sexual heroics it was probably better not to think too much about what he might be up to.

For my own part I certainly never saw anything odd going on in my dealings with Billy Hill. He was like the legends that sprang up about him as the king of the underworld. If anything, he went out of his way to be good to me. While I was overseas he introduced me to Marcel Francisci on a trip to Tangier and I would have still been in the gambling game today if it weren't for Billy's brother dying while I was out there with him in Spain.

Billy immediately went home for the funeral while me and Teddy Machin stayed on in his flat. I was surprised to get an earful from my wife when I phoned home.

'What you been doing?' she shouted. She told me about a visit from Chrissie, the wife of her cousin Mick McKenzie. 'She said, "Teddy says they've gone out there with two birds!"'

I was furious with Teddy. It should have gone without saying that we didn't tell anyone where we were going, but in any case, we made a specific agreement not to discuss our visit with anyone. But Teddy wasn't very bright and was a bit like a child in some ways. He could never just keep his mouth shut and less forgivably he was always stirring things up, which would do him no favours in the end.

I really let Teddy have it. I was furious with him. We had never been proper friends, but we had at least been fairly good business associates and now Teddy was really upset. We never properly spoke again.

When I returned to the UK it was to get on with my life. The Krays were on remand, but they were always going to go down. I needed something new and with the help of a silent partner, who I won't name here, I took on a pub called The Steamship, a little place near Blackwall Tunnel in the docks in E14. At the time I took over it was taking virtually nothing. Maybe £40 a week. It was useless. Knowing that I had no chance of being given a licence, I visited my brother Fred to see if he'd front it. He lived around the Norwood area of South London and although I knew he was an alcoholic, he said he was clean. But there were bottles of beer lying around his flat.

'I thought you'd given up,' I said.

'I have,' he said. 'I went in the off licence for a packet of fags and they got a fruit machine in there. I won – but they only pay you in tokens. They were only good for beer.'

To me this sounded perfectly believable and with that I gave the keys to the beer cellar to an alcoholic. I didn't particularly care. The details of running a pub didn't interest me and I wasn't concerned about turning a profit. I did enjoy getting The Steamship ready for the big opening. I threw myself into getting the decoration right and as I was getting about in the West End quite a bit in those days, there was plenty of inspiration to draw on.

Even the toilets were just right. I used to go to a restaurant in Dover Street which had facilities like little palaces with ornate taps and an elegant mirror and I did the ladies toilet in my place in the same style. I was also proud of the advert I put in the local paper: THE WEST END COMES TO THE EAST END, ran the headline. I included a list of top singers of the time from Frank Sinatra to Perry Como and invited people to come and listen to them on the best sound system around. Bertie Summers set up the audio side of things for me. As a jazz fan, he was a perfectionist and made sure the music was well amplified. It all worked and I'm sure part of the appeal was my unrivalled position of having just come out of the celebrated Kray case. It wasn't a bad scalp to have on my belt.

Guests on the first night included friends I worked with who showed up in their Rolls Royce's, Porches, etc, which they parked outside The Steamship. I should have been serving but I wasn't that interested in being the diligent host. It gave me a chance to enjoy myself. The small space was packed out. A few of the local police turned up in uniform and you'd occasionally see a copper's helmet bobbing about. They were as fascinated as anyone else. There were so many faces there that they wanted to see who was about. My pub became the place to go and everyone talked about it – the ladies' toilet attracted particularly admiring comments. A good part of the reason was my connection with the twins and how

I'd walked away. The acquittal had even made it to the national news and people would have seen me on TV.

The Steamship was, like most pubs at that time, tied to a brewery. The area manager told me he had an important visitor coming to see how things were going and asked me to make sure the place was looking good.

'Be here yourself, won't you?' he asked.

I readily agreed and made sure that everything was polished and gleaming for the appointed meeting. I had no idea who this person was going to be and I was not much enlightened when they turned up. Having had a drink with the brewery man, the pair left without even speaking to me. I couldn't see how this was of benefit to me.

The other curious thing was an ad appeared in the paper for another pub and the wording was identical to mine. It all began to make sense when a friend advised me to go and look at this pub, The King William in Manor Park, Ilford. I hadn't actually connected the ad to what I'd been told until I walked in the other pub and saw that it was exactly the same down to the last detail. They'd pinched the decoration and the signs revealed that it was the same brewery. Perhaps they didn't know about my unique selling point, but they clearly thought that if they followed my interior design they could have themselves a similar hit further out east. I might as well toast their cheek with a drink, I thought. The barman looked very surprised to see me approach the bar and very embarrassed. As well he might. It was the area manager.

'This won't hurt you, you know,' he said almost immediately. 'It's too far away.' I told him I wasn't that bothered and, genuinely, I really wasn't.

My focus was living the life. I might have watched the Krays fall apart but now I was letting the trappings of success go to my head. Most of the time I kept on going out in the West End and I didn't serve a single drink to a customer in my own venue. More importantly, I never bothered looking at the takings. The responsibility was all with my brother and thinking about that now makes me laugh. I left an alcoholic in sole charge of a busy pub and I can't say that I didn't even have warning. The night before we opened he disappeared and he was the one who had the keys to everything – from the front door to the safe. When he did at last call it was long distance from Ireland where he had gone with some girl he met in the pub. We had to work around him when he didn't make it back in time for the official opening. I spent much of the day worrying about the brewery coming down and kicking off but somehow we made it. Fred did come back in the end but it was mostly Bertie, my friend from The Regency, who took most of the responsibility for The Steamship.

I would act as mine host in the pub on occasion but I'd always be on the customers' side of the bar. There was something of a sense of power that went with it, which I liked. All I had to do was chat to people and I knew I had a bit of a reputation, which I was beginning to trade off. When I think about my state of mind at that time I realise I was out of control. The Krays were gone and I'd faced them down – and I liked that feeling.

The Steamship was heading for disaster but I didn't care. I had my famous friends, including most of the players at West Ham. Frank Lampard's dad – also called Frank – was a regular visitor, as was Harry Redknapp. A highlight was the day that half of the first team turned out to play football for me at Hackney Marshes. But I'm not so good on the details now – I can't even remember how I got friendly with most of them. To some extent it must have been because I was known in the East End but it didn't work in quite such an obvious way as that. You just got to know people when you looked the part and I had the smart suits, the nice shoes and I was never short of a few quid.

I could be relied upon to do flash stuff. I took the whole West Ham team to a boxing match by coach, but I'm just not that proud of doing those kinds of things. I'm not sorry about it; I just don't enjoy thinking about it because I was drinking so much. It could have been a good business move for the pub, though I wasn't that clear-headed about it at the time and that's not the point. I just can't think of it without remembering all the booze that went along with it and that makes me feel quite ashamed. While I wasn't falling over drunk, I was permanently hazy.

It wasn't long after that night out that I ran into England captain Bobby Moore. He was great, a really lovely guy and he knew who I was. I'd got to know him when some mutual friends asked me to give him advice when a company he was involved with had some trouble from a mob unconnected with the twins. He had also heard about the coach trip.

'You took the lads out, didn't you?' he said. 'Do you want to come to The Grosvenor for this sports dinner I've got to go to?'

And that's how I ended up at the top table during some glitzy occasion with Bobby Moore.

Being on the top table meant we were all introduced one by one and everyone was being asked for autographs by a few starstruck kids who happened to be there with their parents. It was like a roll-call of the greatest sporting names in the football and boxing at that time. Then came, 'Mr Michael Fawcett.' I just felt like a terrible imposter for being there. I knew there were friends of mine that night who were just in the audience and I felt worse when the kids came running up for my autograph. If it had been during the days of the twins and there had been some occasion like this, I'd have stayed well away and I'd have had nothing but contempt for anyone who turned up. I hated being a hypocrite.

I didn't really know what I wanted. Another gin and tonic? Another pair of crocodile shoes and a beautiful bird? All of that. I had become a playboy more than a businessman. But I didn't have solid money. I never really knew how to manage it. That's what happens when, a bit like the twins, you come from a poor background. I'd lift the takings straight out of the till.

I was drifting along, back doing a couple of con jobs, when I ran into a friend called Willy. A good-looking Jewish guy from Aldgate, much admired – but never caught – by Ronnie, he was a long-firm expert. Willy was good company – smart, and a funny Jack the Lad character. He started off in the 'run out' – mock auctions where you got as many people as possible in a shop with a megaphone and made sure they ended up with a bag of nothing.

Willy had a good touch of more than 100 grand and decided to spend it in America. He told me how he'd also bought two plots of land in the Bahamas on an island called Great Harbour Cay. The Canadian mafia had bought the island and the big boss, Lou Chesler, had a guy called Ray Bonafante, who was a brilliant salesman. The Bahamas was much in demand and he pulled in the celebrity crowd, he had recently sold to Gunter Sachs and Bridget Bardot. Willy had got involved in this and asked me to sell a piece of his land when he realised he'd overreached himself. It would be a good way of meeting his contacts and also seeing if I could interest them in buying a plot back or selling it on for him.

I flew out with my family, though by that time my wife and I were together in name only. We were leading separate lives in the same house and we only just about tolerated each other. I was only staying with her for the sake of my boy, but at least in America we would be able to relax and we did our best – in a hotel with five swimming pools. We did some sightseeing in Miami before I had to head off to do business in Nassau.

All the real estate outlets were based around one hotel and Ray Bonafante himself did not disappoint. He looked like a film star with immaculate grey hair and a big cigar. His face lit up when I said who had sent me. Willy spent like a lunatic while he was out there and had made quite an impression on Ray.

'Hey, what are we doing today?' he said and put a load of his expensive cigars in my top pocket. 'Are we island-hopping? Where are we going?'

You could feel his energy from ten feet away and for a typical Englishman like me it was quite something from a person I'd only met for two minutes. I didn't need to think too much as he had an itinerary planned in the next sentence.

We picked up my family and went back to Miami and I couldn't shake Ray off. The sign of a good salesman, I guess. He sold Willy's plot of land and my last memory of him on that occasion is when I decided to take a road trip to New York. I was buying a Greyhound bus ticket from a bad-tempered clerk.

Ray said, 'Hey, bud, you're being a bit sharp.' He looked extremely displeased and the clerk crumbled immediately, apologising profusely and I didn't blame him. Ray's day job was collecting Las Vegas gambling debts for the Mob and his partners were Eddie and Dino Cellini, two top-ranking Mafia guys, who had been sent to London with George Raft. I loved it really; I was so big-headed and accepting of the life that I was leading. For me it was just a grand holiday – stopping in Savannah, Georgia, North and South Carolina and Washington DC. My feet weren't that firmly on the ground. I barely remembered I had a pub to run back home when I stayed at the Park Sheraton on 7th Avenue, the site of the infamous shooting of Murder Inc's top executioner, Albert Anastasia, and took time to go out to Harlem, back when it was considered to be so unsafe that several cab drivers refused to take me. Willy and I were pleased to be able to return Ray's hospitality on his future visits to London.

I returned home to a shape up that started when the Krays went away and was still rumbling on. Everyone was jostling for position and there was an aggressive new language in the air. Strangely, it was different for the twins themselves. Now they were inside, a lot of the old grudges and feuds just melted away. The pair of them ended up friends with almost everyone once they went away – from Fraser to Shaw. Everybody you could think of – bar me. Not that they were enemies as such. I just didn't go to see them and there was never any contact from their side. Yet people around us seemed to think that I owed them something and I felt there was less respect for me. Some of them were thinking, he's not so smart without the Krays around. The Tibbs family, and particularly young Jimmy, were among those who were testing how far they could go.

Chapter Fourteen

FEUDING WITH THE TIBBS

I knew that Robert Tibbs could handle himself when I went out drinking with him. I also knew that his family were increasingly prepared to strike hard – and first. But I was also more than willing to go on the attack. It was a combination which would end in a fight that evening and the start of a long-running battle.

We were with a friend named Frankie McDonald. He was a ticket tout and was really good friends with all the footballers. He still knows a lot of them. We started at The Baker's Arms in Stratford, then a pub popular with footballers. Some silly argument started between the other two.

Frankie said, 'Look, I'm not frightened of you, but if I have a row with you it'll end up with your brothers.' Robert just sneered at him and on they went.

'Why don't we move on somewhere?' I said. We were all little bit pissed and I drove one car while Robert took his own. He was clearly still annoyed, as he kept stopping and starting and cutting into me.

Despite the stupidity, we made it in one piece to a pub run by another friend of mine over in Canning Town. But no sooner had we got our drinks than the arguing started up all over again with Robert insisting that Frankie had the wrong attitude towards him.

The sensible thing would have been not to have had anything more to do with either of them. And these days, now I don't drink, I may have left them to it. But instead I told Robert to leave it out. Then I looked down and saw he was pulling out a knife. I knew from a conversation that I'd had with Robert's dad that he had only recently assaulted someone seriously. I'm not going to say too much about what happened next, but there was a scuffle between the two of us. As the newspapers later reported, he got his throat cut. Robert survived, but that drunken argument over nothing caused mayhem for a lot of people. Everyone was up in arms.

Robert's dad was Jimmy Tibbs Sr. He had a metal yard in Ordnance Road, Canning Town. He also did some work with a fella called Ronnie Molloy, who got 15 years for a silver robbery and Ronnie Moore, who had been a partner to Georgie Walker. Heavy characters, by any standards. It was Tibbs Sr, Molloy and Moore who had stuck up the Krays' name along with Ronnie Atrill and got Joe Sullivan into such trouble.

Jimmy Sr was the father of three boys – Robert and Johnny and Jimmy Jr. The younger Jimmy was a boxer and the twins had once got it into their heads to manage him. His father was afraid of the twins, despite having quite a reputation himself. He wasn't keen on the scheme and on that occasion I helped them through the potential minefield of negotiating with the twins who didn't have a clue about management. They were shrewd about Jimmy Jr's prospects, though – he was a talented boxer who went on to be an accomplished trainer for the likes of Frank Bruno and Barry McGuigan.

Previously, Jimmy Jr had some sort of dealings with a family of real liberty-takers called the Nicholls – brothers Albert and Terry. Jimmy Sr came to me because he was again concerned the twins would get involved. Once more I told him to leave it to me and he offered me a few quid. He seemed very relieved indeed, but it seemed he had quickly forgotten his fear now the twins had gone away.

The Tibbs got stuck into their feud with the Nicholls, escalating their fights until Albert Nicholls only just survived being blasted with a shotgun. They were beginning to think they were unstoppable, not least because they had very good connections with the local police. When the Nicholls case came to court, the Tibbs were given only a two-year suspended sentence for attempted murder and got away with a fine over the wounding and firearms offences.

Jimmy Sr told me proudly how his son Robert and another fella we knew named Billy 'The Bomb' Williams had 'stuck it on a man in The Bridge House the other night. Poor fucker! They smashed his head in.' As a family of scrap metal dealers, all of the Tibbs were strapping men. Very strong.

Jimmy Sr also said that he himself had been visited by the Dixon family – George Dixon was the loser that Ronnie had unsuccessfully tried to shoot on one occasion. Now there had been some fresh falling out between the Dixons and Jimmy Sr.

'I said to them, "My boys ain't cunts, you know."'

It seemed an extreme response and not like him at all. I thought, that's a bit heavy.

It was the same with Jimmy Jr. He had boxed for West Ham Boxing Club and being involved with the game, I shared a story with him.

'I was reading in the paper that Chazzer Chapman won't let you train in there during the afternoon,' I said, 'because you're a pro and it's an amateur club.' I was surprised by the fury of his response.

'Nah, he fucking will, though, when I break his jaw.' I didn't make any comment but the angry answer stayed with me, particularly as Chapman only had one leg.

The Tibbs were like all metal dealers in being friendly with the police. One yard in Bromley-by-Bow was completely staffed by ex-coppers as most of the scrap was actually stolen. Buildings were going up and down all the time and the effect of bombing during the war was still being felt. There was so much being changed that it was relatively easy to make off with material as long as too many questions weren't asked. But the Tibbs now seemed to be less cautious about causing trouble, perhaps it was because they were so strong with the Old Bill.

In fact, Jimmy Sr said to me one day as we stood outside his yard, 'I took a right liberty. I had a lorry load of whisky in here the other night. Mind you, I had the Old Bill in a squad car outside minding it.'

Robert Tibbs was also being irritating, even before we had our fight. I'd had a row with a fella who was known for being quite tasty. Robert kept on warning me to watch my step.

'He's dangerous you know. He'll come back.'

He said it as if it was advice, but really it was like he was having a go at me. None of his fucking business, I thought, nothing to do with him. And then came the night out with Frankie that ended in our violent row.

All three Tibbs brothers joined together against me and they brought their mates too, including Teddy Machin, who was still smarting from the ear-bashing I gave him in Spain and was very pleased to see me targeted. Teddy was having an affair with Chrissie McKenzie, the same woman who had got us into trouble over the trip. He was obsessed with Chrissie and he used to slag off her husband, my wife's cousin Mick. Among his choicer insults were: 'He eats so much he has to go to the toilet twice a day'; 'He's got shoulders like a Guinness bottle'; and 'He never wears underpants'. His openness about the affair would later have fatal consequences for him.

When I woke up the morning after the fight with Robert, I thought at first, what have I done? Right, I've got to face up to it. I arranged a meeting with Jimmy Sr's brother, George 'Bogey' Tibbs. He was also friendly with the Old Bill and I thought I could test the waters with him. Make a peace offering. I met with him at his fruit stall in Leyton.

'What they want to do,' he said, 'is to arrange for you to come round and have a fight with him in the yard.'

I thought to myself – no, thanks! But I didn't say it.

'I'm a bit fed up walking about with a gun on me all day,' I said instead. 'That's why I've come to see you.'

'They're all armed to the teeth,' he said, 'and they're all fed up too. It don't make no difference.'

Within a day my house got turned over by the police. I thought again about the links they had with the Tibbs. It wasn't a coincidence. The coppers had a warrant to search for preparations for war – gelignite and guns. Finding nothing, they left me alone, but still the fighting continued to spread.

I decided to go to Spain. Once again we went as a family, more because I wanted to have my son Michael with me and I knew I would most likely be away for a little while. Driving to Dover, we boarded the *HMS Patricia* and sailed straight into a force-ten gale in the Bay of Biscay. That was an experience but not one I fancied repeating. I knew where I was going – the place I'd stayed with Billy Hill on the coast between Torremolinos and Marbella.

Back in the UK there was another storm brewing. The Tibbs were going around threatening and beating people, largely because they couldn't get their hands on me. They didn't just stop at friends of mine. One victim was the mother of a girl I knew. The mother worked in a pub in Canning Town and they started scaring her. They were making themselves an absolute fucking nuisance everywhere. One of the bully boy Nicholls family was watching that night and they set about him too, just for being in the pub. The Tibbs had gone right over the top. It was like they were taking on the world and making enemies everywhere. As if they weren't mad enough, Teddy Machin was working them up even more, telling them things that would steer them all over the place in search of a fight. Then he was himself shot, much to the excitement of the newspapers.

Teddy Machin slept in a ground-floor bedroom in a flat in Forest Gate, somebody smashed the window and guided by the sound of his snoring blasted him out of bed with a 12-bore shotgun. Fortunately for him, the bedclothes and the darkness lessened the damage, but he still couldn't sit down for a long time.

Now a nephew of Machin joined in. He had just come out of a seven-year stretch in Parkhurst and was not only spoiling for a fight but was stupid too. Somebody took a pot-shot at him and he almost had a heart attack.

The conflict took a new turn when the Tibbs were themselves targeted. There were shootings – fairly bad aims, it has to be said, which did little damage – but more seriously a bomb was put under the bonnet of Jimmy Tibbs' van. The bomb went off when he turned the ignition key, but by pure luck the force of the blast was directed away from the front seat. Another bomb went off in the office of the Tibbs' yard. Firm member Stanley Naylor was also shot at. The attacks served only to make the Tibbs family angrier and more frustrated. All they could see was that they were being battered all over the fucking place!

To make matters worse, a bloke named Lenny Kersey, who I knew quite well, although we weren't all that friendly, called the Tibbs 'dirty pikey bastards'. It was an incident that was to be well documented in later reports and books. Word got back to the Tibbs and Jimmy, Johnny, Machin and Naylor turned up outside Kersey's house where he was chatting with his wife and a neighbour who was holding her baby. They set about him.

It was a furious assault, the Tibbs crew shouting, 'Kill him! Kill him!'

They covered Kersey with 36 inches of knife wounds. Afterwards his face was a mass of stitches and he had big lumps on his legs where the blood congealed. They also cut his back to bits. The scene was one of horror as the women around him screamed and the baby was dropped on the pavement. It was broad daylight in Stepney Green. Kersey survived, though, he was rushed to hospital where he was stitched back together.

I stayed abroad throughout the fighting and, of course, it couldn't be said that I was involved in any of this. Sometimes I stayed with Hillsy in Morocco at his flat in Boulevard Hassan II in Tangier. As he had promised, he continued to get me in with the Unione Corse and we planned to do the card game scam at the casino in Westcliff, Southend. Billy was going to be involved in anything we did in Madrid but he had no interest in returning to England if he could help it and was happy to leave it to me and his brother-in-law, Mickey Riley. I preferred to wait overseas until the Tibbs business settled down, but it didn't. It didn't settle down at all.

When the Tibbs firm were nicked for chopping Lenny Kersey to pieces, he was given a few quid not to press charges. They were discharged from the Magistrates' Court and they thought they had got off. But it wasn't the same as being cleared after a jury trial. It just meant that charges weren't being pressed. At the time you couldn't be tried twice for the same offence – what was known as double jeopardy – but they hadn't had the trial.

Kersey went on to win some compensation from the Criminal Injuries Board and apparently the Tibbs tried to get the money from him. For the time being, the Tibbs enjoyed the confidence that came from having a very good friend inside the police.

I knew exactly who it was they referred to when they told people, 'Our Old Bill, when he catches Fawcett he's going to plant ten sticks of jelly on him.' Jelly being gelignite. The idea would be that I would get done for the bombings and shootings. 'He'll fucking show him! He's going to get fitted up. When they get hold of him he won't know what's fucking hit him.'

Mostly I was in Spain, enjoying life. I met a girl out there when I was staying with Billy called Wendy Jacobs. She really liked me – and that doesn't happen often. Her father was one of Billy's old gambling associates and she and her mother were involved in a laundry business he had out there.

If I had any business that needed my attention I would just fly back to the UK for a short period and return to the sunshine as soon as possible. My son Michael was fascinated by bullfighting. He was about nine at that time and together we got to know some of the stars of the bullfighting world. Antonio Galán was a bullfighter and promoter I got to know very well and we even visited his home village with him. An English journalist named Sylvia North heard about my son's youthful passion and she said she would like to take his photograph at a fight. She cooed over him, getting his name and how he was doing some training at a bullring run by the brother of the legendary Antonio Ordóñez. Sylvia sold the story to a Spanish magazine and I didn't think much more of it until I was on a visit home and saw a big photo of my boy in *The Evening Standard*. The local paper picked up on the story and named me as a 'restaurant owner' – which is what I'd told Sylvia North. It was all over the place.

That same night I was in The Lotus, an East End club, when I saw Jimmy Tibbs' best friend, a fella named Frankie Simms. He was a tough silver-bullion robber who'd done 15–20 years.

'Get on the phone to Jimmy,' I said. 'If he wants to see me, he can.' Frankie was practically in tears at the thought of being dragged into our feud. He was very much a Tibbs man – he used to run a cafe for them and he was scared that I might set about him. The more I told him to call Tibbs the more he begged me to let him go. His cousin Jimmy Fleet was there and he asked me to leave Simms out of it. I wasn't daft enough to lay into him anyway – it wasn't my scene and I readily agreed.

Bertie Summers used to go to the Tibbs' cafe and he reported back to me the next day that there had been 'pandemonium'.

'Why?' I said, knowing fairly well what he was about to say. 'What happened?'

'Well, your photo being in *The Stratford Express*!' he said. 'And you're supposed to be in Spain. What were you doing up The

Lotus? They went fucking mad! They were all running around like lunatics!'

A mob of them surrounded Bertie. They were always desperate to know where I was and they weren't going to hold back. But they underestimated Bertie, who pulled out a stiletto and one of their lot, 'Jumbo' Connolly, got it buried in his chest. They decided it was best not to follow that line of inquiry, realising Bertie was a dangerous little git and best left alone. Connolly survived but it was his own fault. Bertie didn't have anything to do with the feud and, besides, he wasn't a big fella. As his nickname suggested, 'Jumbo' looked very much like he could take care of himself.

The Lotus was also visited by Lenny Kersey. He was pissed and had a mate with him. They had it out with a fella who was on the very fringes of the Tibbs gang. This was Mickey Logan, who had once been referred to as a 'poor consumptive cunt' – though he wasn't ill. He must have just come over like that. But whatever his natural condition, he certainly didn't feel too good after Kersey impaled his hand to a table with his knife. Logan reported him to the police and Kersey was arrested. The response from the Tibbs camp was an offer to drop the charges in return for a hefty payment – something like a grand.

This was just the greedy response the police had been looking for. When they got wind of it they told Kersey that while he had only inflicted a relatively minor wound on Logan's hand, he had stitches everywhere from the Tibbs' original attack. Kersey hardly needed reminding. The police said they would reopen the original case against the Tibbs and in return he would get off the Lotus charge.

The police, led by a copper called Wickstead, seemed to be serious about this case. Wickstead was a man on a mission to wipe out crooked policemen. His squad ended up purging Soho of its once all-powerful porn mob and the Tibbs knew they were up against it. They tried to make me personally responsible for making sure that Kersey fell into line. The thing was, I knew I couldn't stop him even if I wanted to. He wasn't a bad fella, but he wasn't a criminal and he had been messed up badly. He was a boisterous, mouthy hooligan businessman – and there were many like him in East London. Years later he made himself a millionaire through plastics and he now has a hotel in Spain. At that time the

Tibbs thought they could get to him by saying if he didn't do what they wanted they would swear my life away for slashing Robert.

The police tried a similar trick. They told Kersey they wanted to speak to me, but they weren't after an arrest. Through Kersey, Wickstead got a message to me: 'We're not the East Ham police.' The distinction was clear. The local coppers might want to do me but Wickstead wasn't interested. Wickstead later wrote in his own book how he decided that the Tibbs were a bigger danger to society than I was. He said that I wasn't part of a gang in the same way. But he left out the real reason for going after the Tibbs – they had the Old Bill straight. The pressure on all of us was intense. Not only had this feud got very nasty indeed but everyone had an agenda and many of them would do anything to enforce it. Wickstead knew it and he offered me a private meeting. I thought to myself, I'll have that. I had a right to talk to the Old Bill – I was being blackmailed by the Tibbs.

Wickstead and me got together on the neutral territory of the Embankment.

'We know you had a fight with Robert Tibbs,' he said. 'They want you badly at East Ham for cutting him.'

I said 'What is it you want?'

'You can be out of it if you're willing to admit that this all started over you having a fight with Robert Tibbs.'

'Well,' I said, 'everybody knows it did.'

'Okay, then. On your way.' That was the end of our discussion. The police did go on to leave me alone – at least for a while.

Early one morning came the swoop on the Tibbs. The gang grassed each other up with enthusiasm and before long some 20 of them had been scooped up. Just a few mornings later they came for me. When I looked out of the window I saw the Old Bill with Frankie McDonald in the back of the car.

'You two,' the driver said to us in the back. 'Don't talk'. This simple request was a physical impossibility for Frankie. He has always been incapable of keeping his mouth shut for any length of time. He gabbled on despite the presence of the very tough Old Bill who had been assigned to us. They were serious about what they did – Wickstead's own memoir would be called *Gangbuster* – and they failed to see the funny side.

'Fucking shut up!' they both shouted. 'Stop talking!'

We set off, but in a different direction to Scotland Yard. We were heading to Tintagel House, a more secure facility in that it was staffed entirely by hand-picked coppers who could be trusted. We were searched and surprised that despite what Wickstead had said, they did seem to be after us. Tout Frankie demanded they return his collection of tickets.

'I ain't done anything!'

The police were unimpressed. They told him he could have them back the following Tuesday – three days after the game. Now he was really annoyed and he got a bit lippy, shouting and carrying on. I watched as he threatened to take them on until one of the Old Bill punched him in the head knocking him over a desk.

'You stay there,' they said to me and Frankie was marched off.

I later found out they grilled him about the night of the fight with Robert. Once they had every detail, they told him he had to give evidence. He refused.

'I'm frightened.'

'Who are you scared of?'

'The Tibbs.'

'You frightened of Fawcett?'

'No,' he said. 'I've got no reason to be scared of him.'

That seemed to be all they needed. Frankie soon reappeared and they let both of us go. Wickstead was as good as his word. I got a witness summons to the Old Bailey where I was asked to confirm that I'd had a fight with Robert Tibbs. Did I do it? They meant had I cut Robert's throat.

'No.'

That was as far as my involvement was supposed to go, though they did try and push it in examination. At times it was as if I were in the dock rather than the witness box.

The defence jumped in to ask, 'Did you try to arrange for Jimmy Tibbs to be managed by the Krays?'

Again, I said, 'No.' That was as far as my involvement in the case went.

Evening Standard

02.05.07

The short list

ONE THING YOU REALLY SHOULD KNOW

SMUDGE GALLERY

117 Commercial St, E1 (020 7247 9004)
If you're a fan who can't afford the kind of prices realised at Sotheby's recent Contemporary Art sales, you could do worse than dropping into this tidy little gallery at Spitalfields market. For under £100 you can buy large-scale photographic reproductions of the East End cheekster Banksy's iconic guerrilla art, block-mounted on canvas. Although Banksy has not endorsed the prints, his followers may be grateful for the service, as many of the originals have long since fallen foul of zealous graffitti teams. **CHRISTINA MADDEN**

PSST! WANNA BUY A BANKSY?
VISIT SPITALFIELDSARTMARKET.CO.UK

SMUDGEGALLERY.COM
SPITALFIELDS ART MARKET
117 COMMERCIAL STREET, LONDON E1 6BG

The type of write-up we were getting that upset the hypocritical Banksy.

Billy Hill at work

Keeping a low profile in the 70s

Terrible Teddy Machin

With title contender Micky Driscoll

With Barry McGuigan, a great role model to any aspiring young athlete.

184

With Trevor Curry, British heavyweight champion and Errol
Christie, a great fighter and a really nice guy.

At the weigh-in and ready for action.

Banjo, Patsy Quill, Jimmy Quill and myself at a weigh-in at the Ruskin

Gloving up Banjo

With Patsy Quill and Shane Banjo

186

My great friend Gilbert Acuna (centre) training in America
with Roberto Duran and Sly Stallone.

With my good friend Wag Bennett

Myself with Barny Eastwood and Paddy Byrne, Barry McGuigan's manager and trainer.

Don King, myself, my business adviser and Larry Holmes, recently crowned world heavyweight champion.

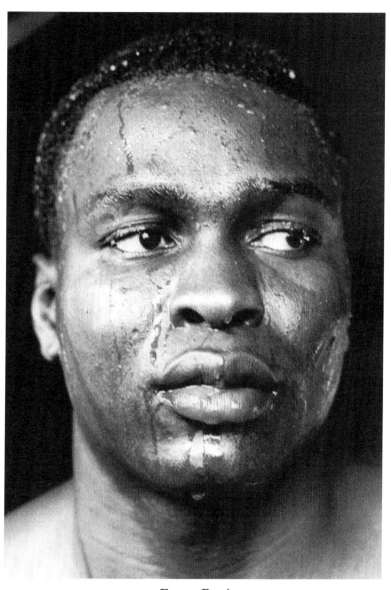

Funso Banjo

Bone Crusher and myself at the Bruno weigh-in.

George Prendas, Marvis Frazier, myself, Larry Frazier and Smoking Joe Frazier Jnr.

Chapter Fifteen
THE END OF THE WAR

I was flat on the pavement in Brussels surrounded by gendarmes with guns pressing on the back of my neck. Makes a change from English coppers, I thought. One of my friends, who had most of the dodgy travellers' cheques in his pockets, managed to escape. The rest of the gear was in the car boot and that meant at least the two of us left weren't holding. All I could see was a whirl of green capes and caps as we were rushed off to a police station. In Belgium they followed the Napoleonic system – you were guilty until you were found innocent.

My brush with the European justice system meant I was not in the UK to see the Tibbs get sentenced. I had gone abroad to do a bit of work, which was all going badly wrong, and I was going to find myself staying away much longer than planned.

I had left London during the trial with some £50,000 of travellers' cheques which were stolen or forged, something like that. There were three of us taking the cheques to Brussels in the boot of my car. Patrick was one, nice enough, and the other fella was an old colonel type. He planned to get money for the cheques in the currency bureaus over there, but he was a proper piss artist. We had no sooner arrived at a car park in the capital to park my Fiat 124 sports car when he started getting impatient. He claimed he wanted to start work but as a real alcoholic, that was just another way of saying he was keen to start boozing. My attempts to decipher the no parking signs were not fast enough for him.

'Come on, there's a space there,' he said. 'What are you hanging about for? We'll come back for it later.' I had parked in a strictly no parking area.

We moved from one Bureau de Change to another, collecting cash at each until, without warning, we found ourselves arrested and in the local police station. Before we could get to the examining magistrate, a policeman came to record the case. He put a sheet of paper in the typewriter.

'Come on,' he said in French. 'What's your story?'

'I've got nothing to say,' I said. They swiftly installed me in a real piss-hole of a cell. It was horrible. The bedding was filthy and it was clear they knew what they were doing. The police had slung me in the worst place they had to soften me up a bit.

After a grim night we got to see the examining magistrate in the morning. Now I had an interpreter.

'I don't know what it's all about,' I said. 'I only just met these people.'

The magistrate had good if heavily accented English.

'I will be looking at this case very, very carefully,' he said. In the meantime we were sent on remand to Brussels' Forest Prison. The regime was very different to anything I'd experienced in the UK. At 5.00 am they would come storming down the landings, pounding on the doors of those who were due in court with their batons and yelling, '*Palais! Palais!*' That meant you were due back in court again at the Palais de Justice. I repeated my story.

'We've found almost £50,000 of travellers' cheques in the boot of your car,' said the magistrate. I wasn't asked for a plea, but was simply bundled back off to prison to await sentence. When it came it included a period '*avec sursis*' – suspended, depending on good behaviour. I can't claim Belgian jail was an enjoyable experience but looking back on it, the time was at least at first, quite interesting. I read *The Day of the Jackal* by Frederick Forsyth. The plot to kill de Gaulle in France suddenly seemed to be all rather relevant and I could daydream the story with me as Edward Fox's cinematic portrayal of the Jackal.

I was there over Christmas when another inmate spoke to me on the exercise yard and I was caught answering. My punishment was to spend Christmas Day in a cage, staring at the walls and thinking what a fucking idiot I was to finish up here.

Eventually I was transferred – by a connecting tunnel – from the Forest to St Gilles Prison. Some of the other prisoners I got to know in Forest were looking forward to meeting up but I ended up in solitary. This was the *étrangers* section for foreign prisoners and it was even more restrictive than the other jail. There wasn't even a proper exercise yard. Behind the gates I'd been waiting to open expecting a bit of fresh air there was just another cage – larger than the punishment cell, but still little more than an extension of the regular cell, surrounded on all sides by netting. I could do nothing but walk up and down, bored to death. Nothing was provided to break up the tedium. No newspapers, no books and correspondence was limited.

Someone wrote a letter from home to say how things had gone in the Old Bailey which – when it at long last arrived – revealed the stiff sentences the Tibbs received. As for me, I wasn't going anywhere. They said that my passport was irregular in some way but I knew it wasn't. The authorities had been talking to the police in the UK and I wondered to myself what they were up to. There was talk that I would be transferred to a prison in a Belgian chateau. It wasn't until someone came over and got a travel document for me from the consul that I was finally released.

Pausing only for a couple of drinks with the fella who got my documents, we took a flight to Southend Airport. My friend phoned someone who met us in the car park where we were shortly afterwards also greeted by special branch with their own brand of welcome home message – a warrant for my arrest. 'Causing explosions with intent'. They were talking about the bombs in the Tibbs' van and office.

'Look, I've been to the Old Bailey over this already,' I said.

But it was no good, they said they had to contact the officer who had issued the warrant. The name was Tom Lamont and I recognised it as belonging to the policeman looking for me over the Tibbs business. I had to admit he was determined. Obsessed, more like. With a name like that he sounded like some kind of fucking Canadian Mounty, determined to get me at any cost. But there was not one shred of evidence linking me to the fighting. How would he prove the bombings weren't the work of any of the many people the Tibbs had attacked? Perhaps more importantly, I had already appeared in the trial against the Tibbs as a witness. Commander

Wickstead had made the decision to go after them and squared that with the director of public prosecutions. Wickstead's side knew that they would have to let charges against the Tibbs' enemies go as the price of putting the gang away. The last thing they wanted was a policeman who was friendly with the Tibbs messing up that result. I outfoxed Lamont the Mounty and they had to let me go.

The mood should have been one of celebration but when I returned to my home in the East End and my regular existence, I was at a low ebb. The adrenaline of the fighting had gone. I no longer had to travel between Spain and the UK. While living abroad my wife had begun to develop the illness that led to her needing lengthy treatment on a dialysis machine. I had been staying with her because of our son but I knew I couldn't leave her while she was so seriously ill. I was trapped in the relationship and I didn't have the security of knowing what I was going to do for work.

Having saved nothing I had gone through almost all my resources and I was virtually skint. What money I did have I was spending on booze and nightclubs. Those who hadn't deserted me in the middle of all the trouble were now fast losing respect for me. Nothing was ever said to my face but people just started to stay away. The consensus was I was a troublemaker who shouldn't have got involved with the Tibbs in the first place. Worst of all, my reputation had sunk in the eyes of Billy Hill. I heard it through Jimmy, the friend I had introduced to Billy and who had got close to him.

'I don't want to know,' Billy said. 'I don't want anything to do with that East End business anymore.' Billy thought I was showing myself up as a terrible hooligan and a generally risky character.

This was an impression that Michael Machin's uncle Teddy did his best to exaggerate. Teddy hadn't forgotten the row the two of us had in Spain and while it was true that I had a real rant at him, he seemed intent on doing his best to get me back by having me killed or, which was even worse, have me put away for life. He had once been the one to introduce me to Billy Hill but, ever the mixer, he was now was in a prime position to make things very difficult. Billy let me know what was happening.

'Ted's been up here,' said Billy. 'He's been telling me terrible things about you.' He gave me a very thoughtful look.

'He's telling everyone, Bill,' I said quietly. 'He's talking to everybody.'

Billy was animated. 'But terrible things! *Terrible* things.' I didn't ask what Teddy was saying because I knew. This went back to some idle banter I'd had with Teddy when we were still on speaking terms. Along with another friend we had been speculating about what would happen if Billy got kidnapped. Who would he go to for the ransom? That sort of thing. It was stupid stuff which Teddy reported back as if it were a real plan. Someone else told me that Billy was now too scared to show his face in the East End, particularly as things had got so heated with the Tibbs. It did seem like anything could happen and kidnapping was something he might well have done himself in his earlier days. Maybe it seemed a more realistic prospect for someone like him. I knew I had been tactless to talk like that but then Teddy shouldn't have been stirring.

Teddy had also got in the habit of telling people that I was going to kill them. It was a bit much and, if only he stopped to think about it, he'd have realised it was a dangerous game for someone who had his kind of sexual secrets. He knew my nature and must have been very stupid not to guess what you probably already have – that word of the affair he was having with Chrissie got back to Mick McKenzie. There's an old Sicilian saying – 'A word in the right ear can make or kill a man.' It wasn't long after the affair came out that Teddy Machin was blasted to death with a shotgun. It was Mick's own relative, Alan, who did the shooting and he got just three years for it.

This did nothing to improve the opinion most people had about me. They thought I was a nuisance and, to be quite honest, I was. I was starting to resemble any one of those idiots who surrounded the Krays in their last days – I was exactly the kind of person I would once have kept right away from. And, what was worse, I knew it. The insight into what was wrong should have acted as an incentive to change, but it just made me feel more depressed. For someone like me, who at the best of times is not gregarious or convivial, I was even more of a loner.

One of the clubs I went to at the time was The Room at the Top, in Ilford. It was after one very typical evening there that I woke up with my bed surrounded by police. That wasn't so typical.

'Come on, get dressed, you're nicked, mate.'

'What for?'

'You'll find out. Get downstairs.'

They searched the house thoroughly. They even picked up a lighter shaped like an antique pistol to examine it closely.

Superintendent Frank Cater, who had been on the Kray case, said, 'May I use your telephone?' They were obliged to ask and I said he could. 'We've got that man,' he said to whoever picked up. They found nothing in the house and, none the wiser, I was taken to City Road Police Station where I spent the night without anyone talking to me.

When I was taken upstairs by a policeman he gave me an apple.

'I bet you're a bit hungry and thirsty down here, aren't you? You've been here quite a while.' It was a softening up trick. 'Those Tibbs are bully boys, aren't they? Fucking bully boys!' He was nice enough, but the attempt to find a weak spot in me was obvious.

The man waiting to interview me was a Commander Davis.

Sprawled in a chair, he said, 'Fuck me! There ain't nothing of you. The stories I keeping getting told I thought you were going to be a fucking great gorilla of a man. How come you're going around setting about all these people and all the things you've been up to?'

This was the cue for my usual response. 'What've I done?'

'Cutting people and all that.'

'Who've I cut?'

'Robert Tibbs.'

I didn't respond. I suddenly realised that I was already saying too much. I thought, I've been lured in here! I'm talking. That was the end of the interview from my point of view. But this was a serious attempt to get at me and I knew the Tibbs had something to do with it. Confirmation came when they came to take me out to charge me and I was surprised to see Johnny Davies and alongside him three other fellas called Jimmy Fleet, David Storey and Johnny Ennifer. As far as I knew, there was nothing that connected us here, particularly not Ennifer, who I think was married to Nancy, the daughter of Bogey Tibbs. Nancy and I got on all right. The Tibbs gang had become obsessed with getting me. They had recruited anyone they could find to help get me arrested. That's why Ennifer was interesting. I didn't know him at all. What's he doing here?

I wondered to myself. This was an attempt to link us as a gang. I thought the war was over, but someone had forgotten to tell the other side.

Johnny and I were charged with attempted murder and grievous bodily harm relating all the way back to 1961, some ten years earlier. The police had dug out The Hammer Club business – the shooting in the bollocks and the rest of that fight with the Bennetts and their mates. I was also charged with beating up Albert Yellop more recently in The Steamship. They said I'd given him such injuries that he had to spend three months under the hospital. Someone was digging deep. I couldn't say exactly why the old stories had resurfaced now – perhaps the police had split over the two sides of the Tibbs war.

I knew that Jimmy Fleet and Davey Storey had once been beaten by the Tibbs, making them automatic suspects for wanting revenge. Ennifer was the odd one out. He was just unfortunate enough to be with them when all three – so the charge went – caused grievous bodily harm to someone in another Ilford nightclub. It was an attack unconnected to me and Johnny, or the Tibbs mob, but by grouping a few of us who had a grudge against the Tibbs, the police made it look as if we were a gang.

We were remanded to Brixton Prison and my first few days were spent on A wing. I'm going to get about 15 years here, I thought – I fucking don't fancy this much. Johnny Davies was alongside me and, as quick to despair as he was to anger, was saying all the things I was just thinking. He operated totally on instinct, wild one moment and tearful the next. The prison made him fearful and he angrily blamed me for everything.

'You go around causing trouble all the time,' he said. 'I'm going to keep away from you if we ever get out of this.' His moaning and whining were constant and I kept sounding positive, though I was worried myself.

Johnny had met a girl – he kept calling her 'sweety pie', which sounded strange coming from a heavy-set gorilla like Davies – who visited him regularly.

Eventually I was moved, along with the other suspects, to E wing, a special block where they put high risk prisoners such as terrorists. The Price sisters, Dolours and Marian, were imprisoned on IRA-related charges.

When we first recognised them, Ennifer started yelling at her and I said, 'Stop your fucking noise.' I think that was the only time I spoke to him. Having had time to think about why Nancy Tibbs' husband should have been thrown in with us, I had come to the conclusion that the police were hoping I'd go for him. As someone in the Tibbs' camp he would then turn and give evidence against me. I made sure I kept my distance unless it was absolutely necessary and then I was careful to be extremely polite.

Our court appearance came a month after we arrived. I was still reassuring Johnny Davies that we would get off but even I was surprised when the magistrate inexplicably gave me and him bail. There was some muttering about it being a gang matter from the magistrate's side of the court and when the other three in our case were pointed out to him, he simply remanded them in custody. I began to understand Ennifer's involvement when he spat in the face of one of the policeman. As they were taken away I was told he was shouting at Supt Frank Cater and from what I could make out he was convinced that the police had promised him certain things. It seemed to me that he had counted on being able to give evidence against me for assault.

I didn't understand why we got bail but it was a piece of luck and even Johnny Davies brightened up a bit. We could both see ourselves getting off and I approached our day in court in good spirits. But in the week leading up to the committal I heard my wife's health was at serious risk. Her dialysis machinery had been moved from our home into London Hospital while I was on remand. When the hospital was put on hepatitis alert, nobody wanted to risk another infection when she was already ill. Her consultant asked me if I would be willing to do the dialysis for her. I explained that I had to go to court.

'If you agree to this,' he said, 'you'll have the London Hospital behind you. We'll move heaven and earth to explain why you couldn't be there – as if you were ill yourself.'

He was very sincere and very caring. This was the non-crooked world at its best. I readily agreed and felt there was something rather apt about me being the only defendant out of five not to turn up to a committal that had been aimed squarely at me.

I called a friend that evening to find out how things had gone.

'Don't you know?' he said. 'You've all been thrown out! But the magistrate was going off alarming about you not turning up.'

The Tibbs had been careful to supply all the relevant information to the police, but they had been unable to persuade the Bennetts to give evidence about what happened that night in The Hammer Club.

Jimmy Fleet went on to live off his brief connection with me for the rest of his life. He became a bit of a gangster by proxy without ever doing anything and continued to have a reputation.

He would look very serious and mutter, 'Don't ask me about any bombings and shootings,' for the very good reason that, apart from being given a beating by the Tibbs for no reason, he did indeed know absolutely nothing.

Chapter Sixteen

BACK IN THE RING

Boxing had been my obsession when I was young. Rediscovering it in my 40s gave me a focus and a new purpose in my working life. I would train fighters who would spar with the likes of Frank Bruno and Trevor Berbick. And as an outsider I would have to take on the boxing establishment, who fiercely defended their interests. Most importantly, the sport helped me give a sense of direction to my own son.

I had sunk back into a familiar state of depression when the fuss around the Tibbs and the trial finally died down. My son Michael was approaching school-leaving age and had no qualifications at all. When we were in Spain I would leave him there when I had to come back to London. I worried that after school he'd end up hanging around outside the bookmaker's and get into trouble. I had to do something about this.

I gave up drinking entirely in the end. I was just fed up – it held nothing for me. I wasn't going to any interesting clubs. I had been getting drunk of a weekend and then starting work again on a Monday. Now I started to take an interest in business for the first time. If you had asked me up to then what I did with my money, I would shrug. No idea. I spent it and I didn't care, but it changed when I realised my son needed guidance.

Michael did his bit to help me too, talking me into getting fit. We went to a gym in Forest Gate owned by Wag Bennett, the man who adopted Arnold Schwarzenegger in the UK. Wag got the future governor of California to give us a brief seminar on bodybuilding. The Hollywood superstar Arnie sat in the informal session and took questions from us few local lads on everything from steroids to workout routines. I didn't realise at the time that Schwarzenegger had previously had an affair with Wag's wife, but then Arnold wrote about it in his own book much later and Wag got sulky when I said, not knowing what was in it, that I planned to read the memoir. But back then all I knew was I was getting to be the fittest I had ever been.

I was at a physical peak but if I didn't have a clear idea of what I was going to do with myself. I knew I needed to make some money. I saw other people buying and selling surplus goods and one of my wife's relatives had a stall down Queen's Road which wasn't doing so well. I suggested to him that if I arranged finance we could try moving it on a bigger scale.

We trawled the Yellow Pages for companies that might have gear surplus to requirements in return for cash. The result was an interesting conversation with the owner of an Aldgate factory which churned out the latest in shoe fashion. Their problem was they couldn't shift the shoes once the tastemakers had moved on. And they couldn't tell when demand would disappear. It was like a tap turning off – without warning they would be left with a warehouse of unsellable gear. From high heels to ballet shoes they were bundled into parcels tied up with string in this massive space. They'd been there so long, said the owner as he showed me a magazine, 'they're coming back into style'. This was exactly what I was hoping to hear.

I soon had 30,000 pairs of shoes and got busy with a stall in Petticoat Lane near Spitalfields and another down Queen's Road. This was the old enemy territory and I wasn't particularly popular, but I didn't care. My back was against the wall and I quite liked it that way. The shoes were stored in an old club we found through a friend at 127 The Grove in Stratford. It had been converted into the world's tiniest car dealership with room to show off just one big car at a time. The space was used for the car finance scam – the zump up which Reggie had been such a fan of. My friend asked for a nominal rent and the place was soon filled with ladies' shoes.

The Grove became another handy location to sell from. And those shoes were soon selling. I smartened the place up, installing the sort of racking I'd seen in my early job back at the Minories. It was exciting as that job back in the Aldgate days had been. I bought a load of jeans, which went out on the new shelving. Shopfitters ended up coming to me and I was soon negotiating rates with signwriters and workers installing blinds. The business needed a name and it was provided by my friend Kipper Turner. I called it Kippers.

Punk rock had broken; *God Save the Queen* by the Sex Pistols was a hit and, with their music playing in my place, the kids in the area started calling it the soul shop. Our shoes were even a big hit with the Chelsea set; my friend Troy, a West Indian guy, had a shop on the King's Road and was selling them like hot cakes. He had a young assistant called Yasmin, a very nice young girl who went on to become creative director at Miss Selfridge. I spoofed antiquarian book shops by placing an advert for 'antiquarian shoes' in *The Sunday Times*.

But it was the publicity from an article in the John Blake column in London's *The Evening News* which really made the place. I realised how successful it had become when shoppers said they had made a special trip from Bristol.

It couldn't last and I wasn't interested enough to keep it going. In time I ran out of shoes and other goods and I was never good at routine. Everyone was enjoying the place so much it seemed appropriate to stop the party while it was still in full swing.

My thoughts were, anyway, turning towards wholesale. Now I travelled around the whole of the UK, bartering and doing deals. A friend helped me out with tough negotiations. I was too vain – I wanted to be nice to people and get their respect. He was the sort of bloke who would tell someone their goods were rubbish just to get the price down. I was horrified to hear what he called one company's stock.

He said, 'Mick, how do you think we're going to buy it for no money if I don't insult it?'

Me, I couldn't do that. I was never cut out to be a dealer.

It didn't matter that the business wasn't for me in the long term. The point was, I was up and running again and I was ready for the chance encounter which led me back to the world of boxing. I had always stayed a fan of the sport and though I hadn't participated since my days as a schoolboy boxer, I had become friendly with some of its famous faces.

Flamboyant US boxing promoter Don King was a great character; he was on a scouting trip to the UK when I met him in 1978. I had a meeting with him in The Churchill Hotel and he brought with him Larry Holmes, who had recently defeated Ken Norton to become heavyweight champion of the world. Don told me he was interested in John Conteh and asked me various questions about Micky Duff, who he constantly referred to as 'the Duffer', but I couldn't help him. I'm quite proud to be still friendly with him. He sent me from America some great photos of me, him, Larry and my business adviser, who I had with me that day.

But it was my friend Jimmy, who I had introduced to Billy Hill, who first made me think that perhaps I might have a go at getting into the boxing game.

Jimmy used to go to Belhus Park Boxing Club to the east of London and said, 'I saw a boxer and I'd like you to have a look at him. He's got something about him – he's a bit different to everyone else.' The fighter was a fella called Babafunso Banjo and he was the son of a Nigerian chief.

At that time Banjo was the ABA – Amateur Boxing Association – heavyweight champion of Essex, but that didn't mean anything at all. Anyone could join their local club, get a medical card and start fighting. It was only when boxers are ready to turn pro that they get proper management. When Banjo boxed for Eastern Counties against Southern Counties he had a very good fight with a boxer called Joe Awome in Woking but lost on points. I was interested and went out to Belhus Park where Banjo told me how he had been amazed to pass a TV shop and see his Woking opponent boxing in a televised match – the final of the Commonwealth Games. The other fighter went on to win gold and that convinced me that Banjo had something. This could be worth exploring.

I went to see him box in Ipswich where he was up against a policeman. He headbutted him and was disqualified. Not a good start. But I knew he had problems with bruised ribs and the policeman repeatedly targeted them. Even in such a poor contest I could see that he was fast. He had the perfect physique – he was 6ft 5 with broad shoulders, good muscular build and fast reflexes – he was the biggest of three brothers. Without having been in boxing long, he was showing himself to be a natural talent.

As I started out with Banjo, I was able to call on some pretty big names for advice about my new direction. I still saw some of the old footballing crowd and was able to ask no less a man than England captain Bobby Moore for some pointers.

He felt he didn't have much to offer and said to me, 'Mick, what do I know about boxing? Mick,' he said, 'look, all I can tell you is what I say to the lads when we're coming out for the second half. I hear them say, "Right, let's carry on from where we left off!" I say to them, "No, no, no. Let's go back to the beginning and start again." And that's all I can say to you.'

I took a lot of notice of that and I found it works. Never take things for granted.

I put my heart and soul into training. At last I had found something I was interested in. But I soon discovered that Banjo was the most difficult person I'd ever worked with. Even the very fact of being a boxer was something that he seemed to struggle with. This was a challenge and I accepted it. And where else did I have to go? I could continue with the buying and selling but this seemed to be an opportunity to make my fortune. My dreams were filled with success and luxurious apartments in Paris and New York.

The work might have been harder than anything I'd done before but it was exciting. Banjo lived east of Ilford in Seven Kings where we would go running in the park. He was hard to get going in the morning but I stuck with it. I knew that if it had been me I would have been out running at about 6.00 am but I couldn't get Banjo out of the door before 8.30 am. And that was when I was lucky. This made creating a programme very difficult but I wasn't put off. Having had to work around personality flaws the size of the Krays', I had all the psychological preparation I would ever need. At least my life didn't depend on Banjo's daily mood swings.

At that time, some 30 years ago, there wasn't so much known about the science of sport and our regime was very simple by modern standards. Fighters spent most of their day in the gym and if you started off with a training run you should have ideally rested before you went into the ring in the afternoon. That was why it was better to be running first thing in the morning. Banjo knew the reasoning behind early starts but his eye wasn't on being the best he could and he would have been the first to admit that he loved clubs like Stringfellows, chasing girls, Chinese restaurants and talking with his friends late into the night. He thought he was God's gift to women and, unfortunately, so did a lot of women. At heart he was a real night bird and that was disastrous for training. At 22 he was, as Jeff Powell put it, just an ordinary young man. But you needed to be a monk in your dedication to boxing if you wanted to be a success. How much did Banjo want it – need it? He was privately educated from a well-off family and his looks meant he didn't need to try too hard.

I found Banjo a gym in North London and would drive him and one of his brothers over there every day. The gym was based on the side of The Wellington pub in Highgate and was run by John Conteh's manager, George Francis, along with trainers such as Joe Devitt. It was an old-fashioned establishment that attracted some of the greatest names in the business, including world light-heavyweight champion John Conteh, trained by Francis himself, recent Commonwealth champion Joe Awome, Lottie Mwale, Cornelius Boza Edwards and John 'The Beast' Mugabi, then in training for a world title. Top class African fighters for Banjo to measure himself against, there were no entry requirements at The Wellington, as long as you were a professional boxer– we just turned up, paid a nominal fee and started work.

Banjo was very tense to begin with and it was a struggle to get him to loosen up. It was his vanity again. He was focusing on the punches that might damage his looks when I knew he could endure more pain than most if he put his mind to it. But he was trying too hard to keep his opponents at bay. George Francis was unimpressed by his attitude. Nevertheless, he did tell me that promoter Mickey Duff had a fighter coming over from Germany called Bernd August. They wanted George to work with him while he was over here.

'He's about your bloke's size,' said George. 'You can spar with him.'

They broke the ring.

Bernd and Banjo were both so huge that the ropes couldn't take the constant punishment from them crashing into them. Now Francis could see what I had seen.

'You've got something there, son,' he said. 'Whatever happens – don't let him get away from you. They'll all be after him.'

Not only very helpful, Francis became a good friend in time. He had a lovely house in Highgate and, as I would discover over the many years I spent in boxing, he was very easy to get along with. There were no superstars in boxing gyms. Even world champions were polite and the rings were filled with far more down-to-earth characters than you would expect to find in a fighting sport. After all the treachery and feuding I'd known in my previous life it was a pleasure to meet such welcoming people. It's a bit of a cliché to say that fighters were easier to deal with because they won respect in the ring rather than by chasing it outside, but it was true. Sadly, George Francis's wife and a son both died from cancer later on and he committed suicide.

George introduced us to the young Frank Bruno. He was still amateur and as a teen was worried about entering the ABA championships.

'I don't know if I can take big men's licks,' said Bruno.

I've always remembered his words. I suggested he sparred with Banjo but no sooner had the two boxers got gloved up than they were told to forget it by Joe Devitt. He said that Bruno was just too young to meet Banjo, though I've since wondered how that spar might have turned out. At that stage in their respective careers my money would have been on my guy. Over a short distance Banjo was too much for almost anyone. For the first few rounds he was always exciting, so incredibly strong and you could see it when he sparred with John L Gardner, British champion, who was then training for the European heavyweight title.

Gardner had been sent from Terry Lawless's gym at The Royal Oak in Canning Town. Over there people had been missing property out of their trouser pockets when they left them in the dressing room. Gardner was a gambler and Joe Devitt was going to be training him.

I can still picture that spar in my mind even as I write this. Gardner was in the corner and his game was to burrow forward all the time, but it didn't work against Banjo, who just pushed him back. Exasperated, Gardner eventually took a step backwards and kicked Banjo in the bollocks. They both had their groin cup protectors on but even so – this was the British heavyweight champion!

Banjo also took a step back. 'Do you wanna box?' he shouted. 'Or do you want to fight?'

He was a student of judo and not a bad one at that. Without giving Gardner a chance to respond he swept his legs from under him and dived on top of him. I looked around for something to break them up and quickly grabbed a Courvoisier water bottle off the ring apron. I thought, I'll have to hit him on the fucking head!

Joe Devitt raced over and everyone started shouting.

I waved the bottle at Gardner and said, 'I'll fucking fight you, Gardner, if you wanna fight.' But it was only a momentary loss of control and the two fighters were calmed down.

As peace returned, Devitt jabbed his thumb towards the door.

'Fuck off home, Gardner.'

And that was that – until Banjo went into the dressing room and found £70 missing out of his trousers.

A more unlikely offer of sparring came from my son Michael. He was only about 17 and had accompanied us to The Wellington to watch. He was insistent that he wanted a go but I knew he'd never boxed and I was very reluctant to put him in at first. He kept asking and I thought that he'd seen what Banjo could do and once he'd had a little taste of it he wouldn't come back for more. As Michael charged across the ring, trying to land a blow on Banjo, he was hit repeatedly in the face by Banjo's ramrod left jab.

After the day's training I stopped at a petrol station on the way home.

'I've got a terrible headache!' said Michael.

I thought to myself, yeah, you would have. That'll teach you. But to my surprise, Michael came back the next day. I might not have been happy at first about him getting into boxing, but what could I do? If Banjo didn't turn him off, nothing would. Michael would eventually go from amateur to professional as a boxer and was trained by Joe Devitt – because he didn't want to listen to his dad. Boxing was good for him, tempering him and giving him strength and discipline. I could see the benefits of it, although in the end it proved not to be the career for him.

In the meantime, my main focus remained with Banjo. It was coming up to 1980, the year of the Moscow Olympics and I wanted to get him on the team. Kevin Hickey was in charge of the English amateur team and its selection but I had no introduction to him and it proved impossible to get a contact. Amateur boxing was sewn up by men in blazers and I was coming in from nowhere. In the end, the lead I needed came from an unlikely source. A fella named Mickey Ludwig co-ran a large car dealership in Ilford specialising in Jaguars and the like. He and his mate were always going on about how much they earned, what they spent and their famous friends, who included boxing correspondent Reg Gutteridge. Perhaps I could put their endless boasting to good use.

'Will you do us a favour?' I said. 'Ask Reg to give you Kevin Hickey's address and phone number.'

Mickey didn't hesitate. No problem at all. I was very relieved – time was running out for the Olympic selection process. I already knew that Hickey was based in Blackpool, so while they got hold of Gutteridge I drove up north, having promised to call the Ilford fellas on the way.

Mickey was less cocky when I phoned him.

'Sorry,' he said. 'Can't do it. Reg won't tell us.'

So much for all the 'good friend' business with Reg. I interrupted Mickey mid-apology:

'Can't fucking do it? I'm halfway up the fucking country. Don't make me turn around and come back to find you.'

He knew I was serious. I'd previously had a ruck with Mickey over some comments he made about a friend of mine. When we next spoke Mickey had Hickey's phone number and his address.

I checked into a hotel in Blackpool where I had a shower and a rest and then phoned Kevin.

'I want to see you about a boxing matter. I've driven all the way from London.'

He was a bit surprised but nice about it and agreed to meet me that evening at his house. I gave him a typical boxing manager story. All about how wonderful my man was and how he was ready to take on the world. I exaggerated his good points to some extent, but there was no doubt that his upright stance was made for amateur boxing. Kevin heard my sales pitch and, to my delight, agreed to see Banjo in action. I returned to the hotel with my head full of the excitement to come. It seemed as if we might actually be able to do it. If he got to Moscow, maybe Banjo could go all the way. I could picture him taking home the gold.

Then Banjo got himself disqualified. Again. At the ABA Essex final in Tilbury. He hit his opponent on the chin and knocked him spark out. But the bell had already just gone. I decided to speak to Kevin Hickey but I knew it wasn't looking good. I was regarded with suspicion as a newcomer in the ABA and that affected their perception of Banjo as well. He'd gone along with someone like me rather than take the blazer-saluting route to amateur success. I was right to be pessimistic.

'No,' said Kevin, 'he's obviously got some character flaw. I can't do anything for the Olympics. Not with his record – he's been disqualified twice now.'

Some months later I watched the ABA heavyweight title fight at Wembley. It was won by Frank Bruno – proving that he could, after all, take big men's licks – and I stopped for a chat with Kevin Hickey afterwards. Bruno was still very young.

'You still need a heavyweight, don't you?' I said. 'He's not anything much.'

'No, you're right,' said Kevin. And he didn't send Bruno to the Olympics either. I decided my next move would be to turn Banjo professional.

George Francis said he would back me. But I didn't have a manager's licence and I knew that the regulations of professional boxing meant that I didn't have a chance of getting one quickly. I asked George if he would manage Banjo for a year. My energy was better spent in getting a licence to be a trainer and second – the official ringside attendant to a fighter. What I didn't know was that the board which was to interview me for my licence included the man who brought down the Krays, Nipper Read. He was going to be very pleased to see me again.

Chapter Seventeen

Boxing with Banksy

The envelope from the boxing authorities should have contained my trainer's licence. But no, it was a letter. They wanted me to attend a second interview. This next board was a much more intimidating prospect and I stared down a long table packed with serious faces, including a stipendiary magistrate, crime writer and solicitor James Morton (Frankie Frasier's biographer, whose subjects have also included the Krays) and Kray nemesis Nipper Read. This wasn't really an interview at all. The point was to inform me that after 'careful consideration' they had decided against endorsing the decision of the regional board to grant me a licence.

The key factor was that I knew the Kray twins.

'So did everybody,' I said.

Yes, they said, but 'you knew them better than most people'.

They might as well have said, 'You can't have a licence – good day. Get out.' Nipper Read had seen me acquitted in the Krays' case and walk out a free man. Now it looked as if he had finally got his revenge.

The decision was a disaster for my plans for Banjo. I was now not allowed to enter the ring with him during a fight. But I was the only one who could motivate him, get him training, keep him focused. Nobody else was able to cope but I was willing to stand up to him. We had arguments, I'd shout at him if it was necessary and I wasn't intimidated. I felt I'd got to know something of what drove Banjo and as his trainer I could bring him on. That belief was what prompted me to apply for a licence in the first place.

Our campaign was given a boost by journalist Jeff Powell, who did a brilliant full page in *The Daily Mail*: IS THIS BRITAIN'S ANSWER TO MUHAMMAD ALI?

When I was preparing for the first interview with the regional board, George Francis coached me through the key questions. A lot of them related to the well-being of the fighter in the ring. Common-sense stuff. I had to know about cut eyes and the list of equipment trainers were obliged to keep in their corner of the ring. Obvious stuff – two gum shields, two pairs of shorts, Vaseline and associated items, but there were also a couple of trick questions that nobody could guess from watching the sport on TV or even from being ringside. The authorities didn't give out rulebooks until the applicant won their licence so you really needed a contact inside boxing to lend you a copy.

The first interview, the one before the encounter with Nipper Read, had taken place at the BBBC Southern Area Council and had centred on my current work. It seemed straightforward enough.

'Are you associated with Wilfried Sauerland?' This was a German promoter who had started to work over in the UK.

'No, George Francis,' I said.

'And your fighter, is this the one who had all the newspaper publicity?'

'Yes.'

My agreement seemed to satisfy them and the licence was confirmed there and then – or so I thought. George got his manager's contract for the year and we were all set until that second board meeting stopped us dead. Nipper Read eventually became head of the British Boxing Board of Control (BBBC) but at the interview he didn't say much to me. Morton, who was a solicitor and also wrote Read's biography, did the talking for them.

It would take me a long time to recover from this knock to my ambitions. What I later discovered was the Kray connection had just been a smokescreen, as the granting of a trainer's licence to Jimmy Tibbs proved. He got it soon after being paroled. The real worry for the board was that Banjo would do better than Frank Bruno and that was what was disturbing some very influential figures behind the scenes. Nipper Read's victory merely fitted in with the board's wider concerns.

The full story came out after the actions of a cartel of promoters were later exposed in *The Sunday Times*. Against boxing rules, Mickey Duff, Mike Barrett, Terry Lawless and Jarvis Astaire had come together to ruthlessly control Wembley, the Albert Hall and most of the boxers. They had their eyes on Bruno as well.

A fella named Bert McCarthy – who already had a manager's licence – was involved in a court case with them over managing Bruno. When McCarthy lost the case, Bruno became one of their stable. Bruno went on to become the main attraction at the Albert Hall for a long time to come and eventually heavyweight champion of the world. The activities of the cartel provided a major source of income for the board – at least until Henry Simmons, Duff's brother-in-law, stole incriminating papers from their safe and sold them to *The Sunday Times*.

At the time we had no idea that any of this was going on, though I had seen something similar in Fleet Street's treatment of the sport. I was at The Wellington when Jimmy Young came to spar before his top of the bill fight against John L Gardner at Wembley. Young was at The Wellington straight off the plane – though I don't know why he bothered. He had beaten George Foreman on points and he was accompanied by his trainer George Benton, but he'd been drinking on the flight and he was practically falling asleep in the dressing room while they were getting him ready. It looked like his crew had seen this before, though it was new to me – this was a world-class heavyweight fighter and he was hungover something shocking. They were having to pull his boots on for him.

He was attempting to spar when big-shot promoter Harry Levine arrived, along with a load of sports writers from the nationals. They all lined up to watch while Levine stood on the ring apron. None of them could have missed the condition of the main attraction. Young was being told what to do but he was just covering up and blocking the punches. It was like he was being punched into sobriety – I've seen that happen since.

One of the reporters called up, 'He's not very fit is he, Harry?'

Harry said, 'Did you enjoy your lunch? Did you eat well? Did you drink well? You should fucking worry about his fitness.'

It was clear who was setting the agenda. Though as an aside, Jimmy was particularly lucky – not only was the press on his side, but the fight was postponed for a fortnight. He got fit and knocked out John L Gardner.

So I'd seen the press at work and now I'd seen the promoters. But in the end it didn't matter to Banjo, who was pulling the strings. All he could see was my failure. He lost confidence and began to think I was some kind of shyster. George wasn't ready to give up and suggested that someone else worked in Banjo's corner and we just get him fighting. There was a show coming up at the York Hall in Bethnal Green, which was promoted by Mickey Duff. I took on a batch of tickets for £1,000 as a mark of my confidence in Banjo turning pro. But just as it looked as if we were getting back on the road, George took me aside.

'I've got some bad news for you, son,' he said. He always called me 'son'. He had spoken with Al Phillips, an ex-boxer who was the matchmaker, in charge of ensuring the fighters would go well together. 'I said to him, "I've got a heavyweight, big guy, quite exciting. He'll take £1,000 worth of tickets for starters." He told me he couldn't find anything for me. So I said, "Look, get the ratings out and we'll start at the bottom and phone everyone until we find someone who's willing to take him. He's never had a professional fight – we'll find someone." You know how Al Phillips has a temper. He said, "I'm fucking well telling ya – he's blacklisted! He don't fight here, and he don't fight anywhere! He does… not… box. Do you fucking well understand?" What could I do? They're like that – they're terrible.'

The cartel had the fight game so tightly controlled that it was impossible to get around them but they were eventually forced into an out of court settlement with some of Terry Lawless' fighters over their purse money and the fact that the cartel was against board of control regulations. But the board knew about this and still let it happen. I had no idea what I could do next. I shared my woes with ex Blind Beggar publican Patsy Quill. He could see that I was so angry I could barely speak. It was all so unfair.

Patsy, who was able to be more objective about the situation, said, 'If it will help you, Mick, I'll have a chat with Jimmy and see what we can do to help.'

Jimmy was a friend of entrepreneur Gerald Ronson and a business partner of Bobby Moore. He had a bit of weight about him. And having been a successful amateur boxer himself, Jimmy was interested. He wanted to know who I knew in the game and how to go about it.

I had been watching the sport as I moved through it and knew of Paddy Byrne, the Brighton-based matchmaker for a former promoter called Jack Solomons. Jack wasn't involved with the cartel. Any employee of his was likely to be receptive to an approach by us. Before retiring, Solomons was said to have called the cartel 'gangsters without guns'.

Jimmy, one of those people who make things happen, jumped into his Rolls Royce and drove down to Paddy in Brighton. They reached an agreement and then set up a fully staffed office. We hired the Assembly Hall in Walthamstow and found an ex-ABA heavyweight champion named John Rafferty. Banjo beat him on points. And he kept on winning, though he would still only respond if he was threatened rather than come out looking for his opponent.

Jimmy was meanwhile busy getting friendly with everyone he met in the business and did the first seven promotions for Banjo at the Assembly Rooms. That left only me frustrated that I couldn't do everything I wanted for Banjo. Nobody liked a winner when they were so dull and I couldn't be in his corner to get him going. If only I could be up there I knew I would be able to wake him up. I'd have got him so riled up that he would have gone for it.

Paddy, with his amiable Irish tones, only said, 'Would you do this for me, Banjo, please?'

What Banjo needed was an East End terrier, goading him on. We needed that training licence.

Mike Barrett proved to be the most approachable of the cartel. He ran the Albert Hall and wasn't quite so much into controlling boxing as the others. Jimmy found that he was quite friendly and at last we were able to get Banjo on their bills. He was invited to box at the world sporting club at The Grosvenor House Hotel against Andy Palmer, a double ABA champion heavyweight who was controlled by Mickey Duff. Andy was a big, mixed race guy who had beaten all his opponents inside the distance, meaning before a decision had to be reached by the judges. He made the mistake of frightening Banjo in the first round, who responded by knocking him spark out. He clearly didn't like the look of Andy. It was a very convincing win but the result for us was that the promoters were even less keen to have Banjo fight Bruno. They might even have tried to poach Banjo from us but they knew my reputation.

So I kept banging on about that licence. I met someone in the BBBC who was more friendly than most and had some influence. He encouraged me to apply again and when I heard nothing he said he hadn't seen the paperwork. Someone must have intercepted my letter before it even reached the discussion stage. It was clear that we were trying to break into something that people saw as a lucrative business rather than a sport and that its establishment didn't want outsiders.

It was Jimmy Quill who made the breakthrough. Another friendly board member suggested he go before them on some other matter and then raise the question of my licence on the day. By that time Jimmy Tibbs was a qualified trainer working for Terry Lawless and the board wouldn't be able to argue that they didn't want someone who knew the Krays. Jimmy followed the suggestion and it worked. I was in.

I had my trainer's licence, but the BBBC kept being a nuisance. There was the time I had a big Irish guy down from Birmingham called Paddy Finn to spar with Banjo. Finn was managed by Paddy Byrne and while he was with us was selected to be a late substitute to fight Anders Eklund, ex-European heavyweight champion.

'You take him there,' said Paddy. 'I'll see you there and you can work the corner with me.'

Well, I had my licence now so at last I was allowed to do it. The fight was being televised and Paddy Bryne said he wasn't keen on my tracksuit top. He swapped it for one he had in his bag and as he was older and more experienced than me I took his advice. It was hardly worth it for the time we were there – Eklund made short work of Finn, knocking him spark out in the first round.

Paddy Byrne joined us in the dressing room with Angelo Dundee, Muhammad Ali's trainer. We got on really well.

'Hey, you got chinned!' Dundee joked. Our little party was joined by one of the board members, Bill Sheeran, who showed little interest in the jollities.

I smelt drink on his breath.

'You are a fucking disgrace!' he said to me. 'That top you've got on. Look at you. You only got your licence because people worked hard for you and look at the state of you.' A small incident, admittedly, but that said it all. The official had no idea that the top belonged to Paddy Byrne and, of course, if Paddy had been wearing it there would have been no complaint. The board were just determined to get me for whatever they could. It was pathetic.

On another occasion Dr Ossie Ross, a board medical official had a go at me for having a coloured stripe in the towel I was using. He said that only foreign fighters were allowed to have anything other than plain white towels. It sounds petty, but they took it very seriously.

I didn't let them distract me from the really serious work – training Banjo, who was by now finding that the commute from his home in Seven Kings to The Wellington in North London was getting too much. Far closer was The Ruskin pub in Manor Park. It was owned by Lonsdale-belt winning lightweight Joe Lucy and he had a gym above it. This was much more handy. All the local tough guys and unlicensed fighters trained there, which wasn't quite so handy. Apart from anything else, they weren't anywhere near the standard of fighters at The Wellington – it was as if a footballer had been training with the Premier League and decided to downsize to his local pub team. But Banjo needed to be nearer home so he could still go out of a night and the Ruskin it was.

Joe Lucy was intrigued to meet me as he had heard how I gatecrashed the boxing world. He said he couldn't let us use the gym of an afternoon because we'd need the keys to the pub. We settled on training during the evenings and Banjo was spared the gruelling trip across London.

My son Michael had been boxing for a while and accompanied us on our first session. Michael had also trained at Wag Bennett's in Forest Gate and was now a pro fighter. The experience was helping to give him the sense of discipline that I had once worried would be missing back when I had been feeling so directionless. I was relieved and proud that he was on track and willing to help out. I took along a few other fighters to The Ruskin, though, after all the trouble I'd had with the Tibbs, it wouldn't have been my first choice. My son and everyone knew about my feuds in the area. Michael was, like the others who came with us, a big fighter, though really what counted when we entered a gym in enemy territory was we were serious and knew what we were doing. Another who knew about the feuds was the only non-fighter – my friend Jimmy who knew Billy Hill. He came along to carry my bag – and I thought it best not to tell the other fighters what was in the bag.

As I thought, a few familiar faces were, if not there to greet us, then there to scowl in our direction. A bit older, a bit more furrow browed but not noticeably more pleased to see me. Among them were Roy Shaw and also Bobby Reading, the one who had been half-blinded with a shotgun years earlier and became known as Cockle Eye. I'd long fallen out with him. Then there was Barry Dalton, who was later found with his head blown off in a van, Mickey May – now the trainer at West Ham Boxing Club, Jeff Smart and Patrick Cahill. It was a packed crowd – all the local gangsters, unlicensed prizefighters and bare knuckle fighters alongside gym manager Bert Spriggs.

As far as I was concerned, this was their call. I had never clashed personally with anyone there. To me they were just the Tibbs' supporters' club. If nothing else, I had the security of knowing that this wasn't the first time we had met in recent times and they hadn't done anything before. We met when I was out on a run and I passed a bunch of them. Nothing happened. Maybe it was just because they knew they would have to kill me otherwise I would always come back.

Ignoring the interesting atmosphere in the ring, our side disappeared into the changing rooms after briefly greeting old man Spriggs. I was glad to have a few 6ft 5 heavyweights with me as we started our work surrounded by the local bruisers. We trained in silence, which was broken only when Banjo sparred with one of the other boxers I'd bought along, Liverpudlian Bernie Kavanagh. Banjo chinned Bernie and decked him. Then the locals began to take notice. This wasn't just some aimless iron-pumping session. It must have all looked very real. I jumped into the ring to get Bernie up and he was furious with me, embarrassed that I'd had to help. He shouted at me to back off and that was a shock for the onlookers, who weren't used to the way real boxing worked.

Until then the local hard men might have been planning to intimidate us. Even my fighters, who didn't even know who the others were, could feel the tension clogging up the room. The local crew were used to being a feared prospect but it was then that the balance of power shifted without anything actually happening.

Against the professional fighters the others just began to look more like actors.

When Banjo wanted to weigh himself I took him to the scales on the other side of the room, where Bobby Reading was standing. Cockle Eye literally ran away from us. His mates couldn't really come back after that. At the end of the night the locals trooped out, all in a line, one by one. Nobody said a word and not one of them ever returned to the gym. I hadn't needed Jimmy to bring my bag after all.

But I did need to get Banjo sparring. A Costa Rican boxer named Gilbert Acuna was in this country, a giant of a man and I got him into the gym. One of the few locals still to use The Ruskin when we were about was prizefight promoter Joe Carrington. In front of me he approached Acuna.

'Do you want to fight for me?'

I jumped down his throat.

'What the fuck do you think you're doing? He's mine, fuck off.'

Carrington backed down quickly enough, but that night I got to thinking that knocking out a few of the local mugs might suit Gilbert. Michael sparred with Gilbert a lot as the Central American trained to take on Cliff Field, the king of prizefighters and was in his corner when Acuna won, stopping Field inside the distance and that, really, made him the guv'nor. He became a bit of a legend.

In turn, Acuna introduced me to fellow Costa Rican boxer Jorge Prendas, who was a super bantam, but he was so good he could knock out lightweights, though I only got him one fight over here. It was against Billy Hardy, who was British European and Commonwealth champion at both bantam and featherweight and IBF world title contender at featherweight, and who he knocked out in five rounds. Then nobody wanted to go near Prendas and I couldn't do anything for him. He hadn't really built up a fan base over here in the way that a home-grown fighter would have done.

My hopes remained with Banjo and working out of Ruskin's was just a step along the way to the champions' gym above The Thomas A Becket pub in the Old Kent Road. This was run by Henry Cooper's former trainer, Danny Holland and owned by another ex-boxer. All the top fighters trained here. Future world heavyweight champion Trevor Berbick sparred with Banjo while he was in London and Banjo well held his own with him for a couple of rounds.

The next day the gym was packed. Everyone had heard about the fight the night before, from my friends the Quill brothers to Mickey Duff, and they all squeezed in in the hope of a rematch. This time Banjo more than held his own for five or six rounds against the Jamaican-Canadian contender to the astonishment of all the fight fans present. *The People*'s sports writer Frankie Taylor – a former fighter himself – wrote a piece which I've kept to this day. He said he had never expected to see such a display by an English boxer.

Bonecrusher Smith got the same treatment when he came over to fight Bruno. One of the toughest, hardest nuts you've ever seen, he went ten rounds with Mike Tyson and was a world champion in his own right. Sparring, he and Banjo locked head to head, punching the fuck out of one another. Even I was impressed with what Banjo was capable of. Jimmy Quill, who had become quite despondent with the lack of success, was as amused as me to see so many former critics now being as generous with their praise. Only Banjo's lack of commitment to training meant that he wasn't able to last longer. He still wanted to be the playboy by night and that held him back. If we weren't still being messed around by the boxing establishment we might have been able to give him more incentive to concentrate on the job at hand.

When the night of Bruno's fight against Bonecrusher came at Wembley Arena, I was watching with a few friends as the fighters came out for the tenth round and Bruno was winning on points. I was getting a bit bored, thinking Banjo's sparring partner was on the way out.

I shouted out, 'Come on, Bruno. Bring back Trevor Currie!' He'd boxed earlier that night.

This really seemed to annoy Bruno. He didn't know who'd said it but I guess he thought the crowd weren't pleased. He went up a gear into Bonecrusher, who immediately knocked him out.

The new promoting force on the block was Frank Warren, then rising fast without the help of the cartel. He wanted Banjo on the bill at Alexandra Palace in North London to fight against Marvis Frazier, the son of legendary heavyweight champion Joe, who was also his trainer. Warren offered ten times the fee we received for The Albert Hall and we would be screened on ITV at 9.00 pm, prime time, on a Wednesday. Banjo tried to pull it together in time but he just wasn't fit enough. There was no reason he couldn't have beaten Frazier – he would probably have got a world title fight from it, we had two cruiserweight world champions in Bash Ali and Glen Mcrory as sparing partners for him as Marvis was a small, fast heavyweight and he certainly appeared full of confidence.

After the fight Joe Frazier was to say of Banjo, 'What a body! If he don't make it in boxing he could do well as a model.'

This was Banjo's first fight with me in the corner. It was also the last. A close fight ended on points to Frazier and ended my association with Banjo. I gave him his contract back. My plan had never been to look after a journeyman heavyweight. I always knew when to walk away and Banjo, I knew, wasn't going to fulfil my dreams. His next fight was for the British heavyweight title against Hughroy Currie, a Jamaican-born fighter he had beaten when he was with me. This time around he lost on points. On some level I was glad it hadn't worked out. It was so hard getting Banjo motivated that if we had kept it going we could have ended up enemies. As it was, we've stayed on good terms. He's doing very well for himself and I still see him around to this day. I was pleased for him when his son Ashley recently won *Britain's Got Talent* with his dance group Diversity.

And that last fight I did with Banjo lives on for a completely different reason. It was just such a thrill to be in the opposite corner to Joe Frazier on TV. I shook hands with him before his son and my man started to fight. When I first got into boxing as a kid I'd never have dreamed of that. It wasn't the financial success I'd thought boxing might be, but in other ways it was better than money.

My next fighter would be my last. He came through Gary Davidson, the owner of The Thomas A Becket pub, who had come down with motor neurone disease and had a boxer he wanted me to take care of. Mickey Driscoll was a good professional. He was very different to Banjo, much more enthusiastic but his girlfriend wasn't keen on him boxing and in some ways he was, if anything, harder to teach. He was, as they say, game as a bagel and he could fight like a demon but he'd learned bad habits as an amateur and the thing about boxing is it's very difficult to unlearn those formative techniques. His trick was to rush in and overpower his opponent, which was great for ticket sales and made good TV but didn't make for such a successful candidate for coaching.

We had an extremely successful promoter behind us in the shape of Barry Hearn and Mickey was not a bad fighter. He came from Portsmouth and the local newspaper would run pictures of the two of us taking up the whole back page. In early 1993 he went up against the British and Commonwealth light welterweight challenger Tony McKenzie in Leicester. He lost in a tense and dramatic fight that finished with a hotly disputed decision. The crowd went mad and it was written up as such by Bob Mee, the well-respected *Boxing News* correspondent afterwards. We got a return fight at The Grosvenor Hotel in Mayfair some months later and this time Mickey knocked McKenzie out in the fifth round of a ten-round title eliminator that Don King watched. He was there that night. McKenzie retired after that.

Mickey himself only had one more professional fight. He had been pro for almost six years when he was knocked out in Cardiff the following year and I felt I had to be brutally honest with him.

'I think you should turn it in, Mick,' I said. And he did. And I did too. My dreams hadn't come to anything after quite a few years taking fighters through the system. That was me finished with the boxing.

In the years since then I've moved around the country, spending a year or so in Nottingham and then another in Market Harborough. I had a friend who needed some business advice and really just wanted a partner, although more for support than anything else. I was kind of a consultant for him. When I returned to London it was to find that everyone had gone Banksy mad.

I'd never heard of Banksy but my friend Steve Diamond had. He was a businessman with the nickname Legs, after Legs Diamond, the American gangster. He just didn't have a good grasp of the finer details of business. He was much better at the ideas side and when his Smudge Art Gallery in Spitalfields Market ran out of money, I invested a few quid. I helped to steady his approach. It was his idea to take photographs of site-specific Banksy works and mount the prints on wooden blocks for the home market.

I was good at the advertising side and the business was very successful. Banksy's lawyers were not so impressed.

'We act for the world-famous artist,' began the letter they sent us. They had printed out all the images from our website, which they included as part of their complaint. The solicitor we consulted was a copyright specialist who suggested we give up, but I wasn't prepared to drop out just yet. We went to the next level, a barrister, which cost a nice few quid. Between them our legal team wrote us a letter and the opening sentence was a killer: 'Who is this man?'

You'd need a degree in law to understand the technicalities of the rest of our response, but it had the desired response. Banksy's team must have thought they might have to reveal the secretive artist's true identity and we never heard from them again.

At Christmas, Banksy would locate and take over one empty shop in the West End and rename it The Grotto for the season. I visited with my 'art adviser' just to check out the man's work. Banksy's then manager, Steve Lazarides, arrived and we got to see the enemy at close quarters without them realising it.

The Spitalfields gallery got its products into mainstream retail in America. We were doing lots of business with the company Urban Outfitters. The American firm were keen on a number of our artists until the legal side of things frightened them off. But we were the most profitable company working out of Spitalfields until Banksy went out of fashion.

I've been enjoying a much quieter life since the gallery closed. I'm still with the woman I met at the end of the 1970s and if I've kept quiet about the family side of things in this book, that's mostly because I wouldn't like it to influence my younger relatives or cause them problems. I've seen how that happens.

I never did speak to the Krays again, though I did think of Ronnie in prison. When we were in our prime he always liked to claim that he couldn't wait to get old. He said he was cultivating any white hairs he found and that 'it will be wonderful when I'm old. *Love* to be old, have all grey hair.'

I wonder if the twins ever thought of what a big favour they did me by never talking to me again – and never, ever mentioning my name. They talked about everybody you could think of and my photo is in loads of the books. I often wonder if the reason is that Reggie didn't want Ronnie to find out about the Frances-Levy incident. That has worked out much better than being in their reflected spotlight. The captions sometimes include my name, but more often they say the twins are 'with friends'. I never really knew what they thought of me leaving them.

These days I'm a lot calmer. I think so, anyway. Some of my friends and family think I'm still mad. Maybe I've been doing this too long. I'm very aware of potential threats all the time. Walking down the street, getting on the underground, I scan everyone in the same carriage as me, just making a note of who I don't like the look of. That's me. Perhaps I am a bit mad but I don't think so, it keeps me mentally alert and physically fit.

Many thanks to Claire at Indepenpress for her invaluable assistance in the production of this book.

Printed in Great Britain
by Amazon.co.uk, Ltd.,
Marston Gate.